7 Pillars of Freedom

Dynamic Public Policy Ideas for a Better USA and World

By

Mike Bentley

PRESS

7 Pillars of Freedom
Dynamic Public Policy Ideas for a Better USA and World
by Mike Bentley

Printed in the United States of America

ISBN 9781594679247

www.xulonpress.com

The 7 Pillars of Freedom

1. End Abortion, America's Crisis
(Human life begins at implantation)

2. Eliminate Predatory Criminals and Crime
(Domestic legal reforms)

3. Eliminate Terrorists and Tyrants
(National security and international relations)

4. Enable Prosperity
(Tax and budget reforms)

5. Establish School Vouchers and Universal National Service
(More parental responsibility and a national right of passage)

6. Reduce Health Care Costs and Increase Access to the Health
Care Market
(Health care reforms)

7. Fulfill Promises to Current Seniors and Eliminate Future
Socialism
(Social Security and Medicare reforms)

"Finally, brothers, whatever is true, whatever is noble, whatever is right, whatever is pure, whatever is lovely, whatever is admirable— if anything is excellent or praiseworthy— think about such things."
Philippians 4:8 (NIV)

Introduction

A merica and the world will greatly benefit from these 7 Pillars of Freedom. Too optimistic? Not when you realize the implications—that each pillar, in its own way, provides solutions to life and death issues. Millions of lives will be saved or improved when these recommendations become law.

The 1st Pillar is most obvious. Since I believe that life begins when the fertilized egg implants in the womb, I am calling for an end to post-implantation abortion. The nature and magnitude of this problem (tens of millions of fetal children have been killed in the United States since the dreadful Roe v. Wade decision was handed down by our Supreme Court in 1973) makes it the most unjustifiable loss of American lives in our history. Internationally the death toll is dramatically higher.

My recommendations in the 1st Pillar prohibit all abortions. However, there are unplanned medical emergencies where certain procedures that will save the mother's life will unintentionally and unavoidably kill the child (procedures correctly not categorized as abortions). This single change in American law will protect all children currently killed for birth control reasons—and save more than a million innocent lives per year. I further recommend amending the U.S. Constitution to support this new pro-life legislation, giving it additional strength and permanence.

The 2nd Pillar contains recommendations for reforming our judicial system, changes designed to protect Americans and our guests from predatory criminals. I believe that harsher penalties will have a prohibitive effect on the criminal element—preventing most violent and other crimes and virtually ending recidivism (repeat crime). I recommend that judges screen all cases for merit before they are allowed to proceed through the criminal justice system. And since far fewer prisoners will be entering restitutional confinement, I support reducing our emphasis on incarceration. Those prisoners required to provide restitution to their victims should be placed in productive settings where they can pay literal debts to society—returning value to those they have harmed.

In the 3rd Pillar I recommend national security reforms including building on the pro-active international policies we have now—engaging the world for the specific purpose of eliminating threats before they harm us, and freeing oppressed peoples from tyranny. We must seek out terrorists and thugs (and the regimes that sponsor and shelter them) and diplomatically encourage them to change—or eliminate them by force. This kind of balanced proactive engagement will help prevent 9/11 catastrophes, prevent massacres such as occurred in Rwanda and Yugoslavia, and end the current tragedy in the Sudan.

My emphasis is on preventing holocaust and international terrorism worldwide, and supports current United States policy that advocates identifying and eliminating any group or government that threatens America or our close allies. Ideally our goal should be nothing less than eliminating objective evil from the emerging world—and practically we are the only nation that can protect the world's abused masses or innocent minorities. We should help freedom-loving peoples everywhere to transform themselves into reasonable democracies, and we should remain along side these new friends for a generation or more—until they grow strong enough to withstand the forces of tyranny.

Those working in dark corners to undermine freedom, or to cause these new lighthouses of liberty to slide backwards into slimy pits of oppression, will be smothered by newly independent peoples no longer willing to submit to thuggery and deception.

Yet we must always keep in mind the Biblical dictum to trust God for ultimate victory, and not rely solely on the size of our army. We must lead by moral example as we clean up our own act here in America—this "shining city on the hill". And though we should always recognize and honor our own Judeo-Christian moral foundation, we should also support religious freedom here and throughout the world as an integral part of democratization.

However, a practical and vital component of our proactive international strategy **is** a larger and more powerful military, one that will greatly enhance the effectiveness of our diplomacy. When our State Department has greater leverage, it can more effectively negotiate with friends and allies, as well as with rogue nations and fence-sitters. This is the essence of peace-through-strength, the seeming paradox that will eliminate most war. In the long run, pro-active American leadership will facilitate a more peaceful world.

An implication of a stronger military and resultant empowered diplomatic corps, is increased ability to pressure nations such as China to curtail its horrific practices of mandatory abortion, and their tolerance of female infanticide. In China alone an estimated ten million children are killed annually through abortion, plus an unknown number of baby girls killed in infancy because of the draconian "one child" policy. Terrible demographic imbalances exist because of this pointless destruction of innocent lives.

The 4^(th) Pillar contains two recommendations intended to give our economy its greatest boost ever. First, we should transform our federal tax system from one that taxes income to one that taxes consumption. The Sixteenth Amendment should be revoked and a federal retail sales tax implemented. Part of this recommendation calls for all states to modify their existing tax systems so that they match the new federal system. These changes will magnify many economic benefits and efficiencies.

Second, I recommend modifying several areas of our federal budget. These changes, financed by the new tax system, will within a generation allow us to pay off all of our debts and significantly lower our taxes. In the long run we can also reduce or eliminate many of the socialistic components that have crept into our financial infrastructure and culture. Some of these liberty-stifling programs have been expanding since the Great Depression, and today, Congress still wields the power to take money away from successful Americans and give it to others—the essence of distributive socialism.

There is an old saying that **when government can give the people everything they want, it can take away everything they have.** I advocate changes to our system that will return financial liberty and responsibility to individual citizens.

The 5th Pillar contains a call for mandatory and universal national service for all young adults after high school, and further calls for restructuring our educational system by empowering parents with a substantial ($5,000 per child) federal/state funded school voucher program. This program is not intended to redistribute wealth, but rather to symbolically and substantively transfer essential power from the government to the governed.

The 6th Pillar addresses changes needed in our healthcare system. Recommendations focus on reducing costs associated with malpractice insurance and jury awards, and on creating a specific medical court system to screen and try medically-related cases.

The 7th Pillar is of particular importance to seniors. It contains recommendations that enhance Social Security and Medicare benefits for current and soon-to-be retirees, and provides these benefits (with cost of living adjustments) for the rest of their lives. However, in the long term, I am calling for a phase-out of these two massive entitlement programs, starting with those folks retiring in 2021 and ending with those retiring in 2052. Both programs will cease paying benefits when the last beneficiary dies about 100 years from now.

Current seniors will have more resources ($30,000 for most individuals), and future retirees will have more liberty, dignity, and responsibility to save for their own golden years.

Context

Before moving to a chapter-by-chapter presentation of the 7 Pillars, I want to share a bit about who I am and where I am coming from. Reasonable transparency will provide informative context, and give insights into the origins of my public policy ideas.

This book is being written during the 2004 presidential campaign, and all parties are offering their records of accomplishment and their recommendations for the betterment of America and the world. None however, are offering platforms that are as clear, concise, and comprehensive as the 7 Pillars, nor are these platforms ideologically consistent with what I believe. This situation has reinforced my desire to present my case, and to enter the public policy arena to champion this platform that blends conservative and libertarian ideas. My goal is to save lives, and to help everyone enjoy a better quality of life—both my fellow Americans and our neighbors around the world.

I also want to disclose that I am a Republican—a descendant of three generations of patriots who served our party since it's founding. My great-grandfather, Dr. Michael O. Bentley (1837-1910) cast his first vote for Abraham Lincoln in 1860, and then served as a Union Army medic early in the Civil War. He left the army to attend the University of Michigan Medical School in the hopes of becoming an army doctor, and was able to support President Lincoln again in 1864. After graduating from UM Medical school in 1865, the war was over so Dr. Bentley decided to invest the rest of his professional life practicing medicine in upstate New York. He retired in 1905.

My grandfather, Joseph Edgar Bentley (1876-1934) supported the party as did my father, Charles Michael Bentley (1897-1981). The lone occasion on which my father and grandfather broke ranks with the party was in 1932 when our family (and many others) was in such dire straits. They voted for Franklin D. Roosevelt on that occasion partly because they admired his relative Theodore Roosevelt. But by 1936 my dad didn't like the socialist programs emanating from the Roosevelt administration, and though he disagreed with the isolationist voices in his party, he supported the Republicans from 1936 onward, casting his final vote for presidential candidate Ronald Reagan in 1980.

I have early memories of my parents doing precinct work in our small town of Seaside, California (our part of which later became Sand City after my father helped found a new municipality there in 1960), so the idea of public service was modeled for me early.

I was first able to vote in 1972, and was happy to cast my vote for President Richard M. Nixon. Since then I have supported the party in small ways, always voting for "our guy". I am happy with

President George W. Bush, and fervently hope he will be returned to office by a grateful nation, thankful for his leadership during this especially dangerous post-9/11 era. I also voted for his father twice, and regretted the style and content of his successor's presidency.

So I have Republican roots. But as a party and nation we can never be content to rest on our laurels, or become complacent even when we have an excellent leader. We must plan for the future, and it is my hope that the 7 Pillars will be viewed as I intend them—a positive vision that will build on our current successes. We must move forward as a nation with vision and innovation or we will slide backwards. We can't change the past—only learn from it. Let's learn and apply whatever lessons we can harvest from our sacrificial history of service to ourselves and the world.

Specifically, I like President Bush very much, and appreciate his obvious Christian faith and his courage to lead the country into successful wars against dictatorial regimes in Iraq and Afghanistan. His policies have helped eliminate dangerous enemies and freed millions of people from tyranny. But the president is handicapped in fighting a global war against terrorism with a military that is way too small and under-budgeted.

Even more important, as a fellow Christian I know President Bush wants to stop abortion, but the pro-life agenda is not at the top of the party's platform (in fact, it is not discussed until the very good "promoting a culture of life" section near the end of the RNC's platform document).[1]

I fully support pro-actively eliminating evil regimes and terrorists, especially when considering their capacity to hatefully acquire and use weapons of mass destruction (nuclear, biological, and chemical). But I am dismayed that more children are killed every day during abortions here in America, than the number of those who were killed at either Pearl Harbor that started World War II, or in New York City when the World Trade Center towers were destroyed in 2001. The latter was a heinous act of cowardly barbarism that started this phase of the war on terror.

I hope we have another term under President Bush that will be even better than his first term, and I am confident that he will always strive for improvement. But I believe our party's agenda must be reprioritized, and that ending abortion must become a higher priority for all Americans. The 1st Pillar is dedicated to that end. But we also need a new tax system and other policy changes— each enabling us to better cope with our dynamic and dangerous world.

I hope parts of the 7 Pillar's policy recommendations are adopted during the next four years, and that the remainder becomes law during the following presidential tenure. And though it is far easier to rely on one person or a few leaders to enact for the changes we want, I believe that the only way we can achieve fundamental change is for a majority to get involved. These crucial ideas must be discussed around every kitchen table and water cooler in America, and then acted upon—in other words they must be popular to become law. Without the power of "We the People" striving together to elect leaders that will implement these changes, the 7 Pillars will be overwhelmed by those who oppose them or ignore them.

At the end of the book I introduce the 7 Pillars Coalition, the public policy organization I founded on the basis of the ideas in this book. My plan is to promote this conservative/libertarian platform by means of a political strategy that can rightly be called "populist" in its approach, and I invite everyone who shares these ideals to join me. Our coalition will be comprised of everyone who believes that this set of policies articulate the right direction for the country—a coalition of everyone who will take ownership of the responsibility to push this agenda to the forefront of our domestic conversation. The Coalition needs a core group of patriots who will champion this platform and elect leaders at all levels of federal and state government—legislators who will insure that the 7 Pillars of Freedom become important parts of United States law. (Please Note: In 2006 the 7 Pillars Coalition ceased operations and the website was closed).

The Faith of our Founders

To build on this theme of transparency, of even greater importance in this discussion of context is religious faith. I am a Christian, born and raised in a nation founded by devoted Christians who wove their biblical values and worldview into our Declaration of Independence and Constitution and history and culture. Their biblical faith provided comprehensive motivation for establishing this island of liberty—free of Europe's suffocating class structure. I have a Christian worldview as did most of the Founders, and our laws and political structure were heavily influenced by biblical principles and tradition.[2]

That said, there needs to be clarity regarding the current controversy of "separation of church and state". Most every American has an opinion on this important topic, with views ranging from something close to wanting a near theocracy on the one hand, to those advocating something like an atheistic spiritual vacuum on the other. I obviously don't want anything to do with the latter structure, filled as it is with anti-supernatural bias. But the last thing I want is a theocracy, even a Christian one, modeled anything like the liberty-stifling Moslem states situated in the Middle East and Asia. The only theocracy I long for is the Millennium Kingdom ruled by Christ—but that is part of my personal religious views, not the form of government I advocate for our nation or secular society. I do advocate utilizing biblical principles (as did our Founders) as the basis of our laws.

What is the right balance? The bottom line is that in our society, we can set the bar wherever we decide. I propose that the laws that govern our secular state be based on the traditional biblical worldview held by our Founders—that remarkable group of visionaries who drew on the principles of liberty and individual responsibility that they read in Scripture when they established our republican form of democratic government. These principles are vaguely addressed today as "family values", but in reality, traditional American family values are principally Judeo-Christian biblical values—many of which are also shared by other religions here and around the world.

We in the West must certainly give credit to legal and cultural innovations developed by the Greeks and Romans, and to the Renaissance visionaries in post-dark ages Europe who utilized their Christian worldview and drew from the best of the past and built a vibrant society. But the morality of our western societies came from the Bible, not from the secular humanism of the so-called Enlightenment that followed the Renaissance, a philosophy that elevated the creature above the Creator—the essence of idolatry. Nor did our Founders draw upon the morality of ancient cultures steeped in heathenistic paganism.

However, let me stress that there is a great difference between honoring the best of the past, and retaining and applying Biblical principles in our legal structure and general culture on the one hand, and utilizing our three-part secular government to promote specific Christian worship and theology on the other. An example of balance is in acknowledging that the Ten Commandments are the basis of our moral and legal code, but at the same time, not requiring worship of the Judeo-Christian God or of prohibiting fellow citizens and our international guests from freely exercising diverse morally-based religious practices.

The Ten Commandments are the moral, philosophical, and legal pillars of our society, and should remain prominently displayed on government buildings, and should be seasonally displayed in public places during appropriate religious holidays like Christmas and Easter. Our Supreme Court building is a perfect example of this balance—a visible testimony to both our Classic and Judeo-Christian heritage.[3]

Further application of this balance includes situations where clergy or laymen are asked to give invocations or benedictions at various public events. They shouldn't be required to be (nor forbidden from being) Christians, nor from praying in Jesus' name. This balance is also found in the work of military chaplains, a model I experienced first-hand during my tenure as a U.S. Army chaplain (1980-1995).[4]

This balance does not nullify the freedom of religion we all want in America, nor should it interfere with our efforts to promote religious freedom as a vital part of our general efforts to democratize the world. Rather, honoring our Christian heritage within the daily practices of government provides an objective basis and vivid example of the success of American liberty.

Unfortunately, those who promote a more traditional balance in our secular society, who want to include our Christian heritage in the day-to-day life of our public discourse and practice, face nearly constant attack by the radical left which is trying to impose secular humanism on people of faith who overwhelmingly honor our religious history. There is a great difference between a governmentdirected Christian society on the one hand, and a governmentdirected secular/humanistic society on the other.

For most of our history this balance was taken for granted, and the context of our culture could generally be called Christian. But through complacency, our traditional faith-based culture has been undermined, and in some ways it has been supplanted by antisupernatural bias. Yet it is not too late to retrieve what has been lost, and I advocate returning to a Biblically principled legal structure that was the backbone of our society from its inception, and to the cultural norms that emanated from a people who respected and honored our Judeo-Christian heritage.

I want a society where religious freedom can be experienced and expressed in both individual families and in normal public gatherings—ordinary places such as high school football games where a simple invocation by a clergyperson is expected and honored.

As an aside, you may remember that during Desert Storm someone in our government hierarchy was so afraid of upsetting the Saudi's theocracy that military chaplains were forced to remove their crosses or Stars of David from their uniforms. During my few months' service in the Gulf I had occasions to meet with local community leaders, and I asked them what they thought of this prohibition. To a person they expressed the view that they thought it unnecessary, and commented that if our roles were reversed, they would not want to remove their Moslem insignia's when serving in America. To underscore this point, when officers from Saudi Arabia and other nations attend U.S. military schools, they wear their normal uniforms and insignias when military dress is appropriate.

Let's work together to find an honorable historic balance for our laws and customs—a balance that is a good witness to the world, one that brings credit to our shining city on the hill. I offer the 7 Pillars to this end.

Summary

I am grateful that you are reading my book, and with the foregoing as an introduction, I progress to a chapter-by-chapter presentation of the recommendations in each pillar of freedom. These recommendations are my vision, and if one or more of the 7 Pillars accurately reflects your views, I invite you to join me in championing them until they become vital parts of American law. I believe these ideas will dramatically improve our nation and world.

Notes

(1) Please see the Republican National Committee platform at: http://msnbcmedia.msn.com/ imsnbc/Sections/news/politics/convention/RNC-2004platform.pdf, page 84.

(2) To explain my Christian worldview more clearly, please let me quote from an article in the July/August 2004 issue of *Focus on the Family Magazine*. The article accurately presents my beliefs since my conversion to Christianity in 1971, and apart from my sins, also reflects my life experience as well. This worldview is a vital part of the philosophical underpinnings of my political beliefs, and has guided me as I formed my public policy platform—expressed herein as the 7 Pillars of Freedom.

The article on page seven is entitled "What's a Worldview Anyway?" and is written by Del Tackett. Mr. Tackett explains that a worldview "is the framework from which we view reality and make sense of life and the world. '[It's] any ideology, philosophy, theology, movement or religion that provides an overarching approach to understanding God, the world and man's relations to God and the world.'"

From this general definition, the more specific definition of a biblical worldview is given: "A biblical worldview is based on the infallible Word of God. When you believe the Bible is entirely true, then you allow it to be the foundation of everything you say and do. That means, for instance, you take seriously the mandate in Romans 13 to honor the governing authorities by researching the candidates and issues, making voting a priority." Page 8.

The eight criteria given in the article to confirm a Biblical worldview are:

1. Belief in absolute moral truth.
2. Belief that the Bible defines absolute moral truth.
3. Jesus Christ lived a sinless life.
4. God is the all-powerful and all-knowing Creator of the universe, and He rules it today.
5. Salvation is a gift from God that cannot be earned.
6. Satan is real.
7. A Christian has responsibility to share his or her faith in Christ with other people.
8. The Bible is accurate in all its teachings.

These eight criteria are also interesting because they were part of a political opinion poll conducted by George Barna. In the poll a cross-section of Americans and Christians were asked to what extent they subscribed to these eight criteria. Only 9% of Christians and 4% of the general population stated that these criteria matched their views.

Though my personal religious beliefs are in the minority, I strongly believe the 7 Pillars will have broad appeal. It is in this hope that I offer this comprehensive public policy platform to my fellow citizens—it is a referendum on their acceptance.

(3) Here are some interesting facts regarding our Founder's respect for the Ten Commandments:

1. As you walk up the steps to the building which houses the U.S. Supreme Court, you can see near the top of the building a row of the world's law givers and each one is facing toward a person in the middle who is facing forward

with a full frontal view — it is Moses and he is holding the Ten Commandments.

2. As you enter the Supreme Court courtroom, the two huge oak doors have the Ten Commandments engraved on the lower portion of each door.

3. As you sit inside the courtroom, your can see on the wall, right above where the Supreme Court Justices sit, a display of the Ten Commandments.

4. There are Bible verses etched in stone all over the Federal buildings and monuments in Washington, D.C.

5. James Madison, the 4th president of the United States, known as "The Father of our Constitution", made the following statement: "We have staked the whole of all our political institutions upon the capacity of mankind for selfgovernment, upon the capacity of each and all of us to govern ourselves, to control ourselves, to sustain ourselves according to the Ten Commandments of God."

6. Patrick Henry, that patriot and Founding Father of our country said, "It cannot be emphasized too strongly or too often that this great nation was founded not by religionists but by Christians, not on religion but on the Gospel of Jesus Christ".

7. Every session of Congress begins with a prayer by a paid preacher, whose salary has been paid by the taxpayers since 1777.

8. Fifty-two of the fifty-five founders of the constitution were members of the established orthodox churches in the colonies.

9. Thomas Jefferson worried that the Courts would overstep their authority and instead of interpreting the law would

begin making law...an oligarchy where the few rule the many.

10. The very first Supreme Court Justice, John Jay, said, "Americans should select and prefer Christians as their rulers."

My question is how can most everything we have done for the past 228 years suddenly be un-constitutional? We certainly can respect each citizen's or guest's freedom to practice their religions, whether Christian or not, but this freedom should not curtail us from practicing our Christian faith, nor require us to deny our heritage.

But we shouldn't be precluded from denying freedom to those who actively plan the destruction of our great land either. If your religion compels you to fly airplanes into our buildings and kill our people—go somewhere else—or else!

For additional quotes and information concerning the Christian faith of Founders including George Washington, John Adams, John Marshall, George Mason, and others, please see *America's Christian Heritage*, published by the Center for Reclaiming America at www.reclaimamerica. org. This organization also refers readers to additional resources on our Christian heritage:

1. *Faith and Freedom* by Mathew D. Staver.
2. *The Patriots Handbook* by George Grant.
3. *America's God and Country* by William J. Federer.
4. *Election Day Sermons* edited by David Hall.
5. *Original Intern: The courts, the Constitution, & Religion* by David Barton.

(4) I had the privilege of serving in all five U.S. Army components, including active duty, active and inactive Reserves, and active

and inactive California National Guard. I volunteered for and served three overseas tours (Korea, Egypt [the Sinai Peninsula], and in Saudi Arabia during the Gulf War). During my tenure I most enjoyed my 41 months with the 101st Airborne Division (Air Assault).

"You created my inmost being; you knit me together in my mother's womb. I praise you because I am fearfully and wonderfully made; your works are wonderful, I know that full well. My frame was not hidden from you when I was made in the secret place..."
Psalm 139:13-15a (NIV)

"Woe to those who call evil good and good evil…"
Isaiah 5:20a

CHAPTER ONE

The 1st Pillar of Freedom: Human Life Begins at Implantation

From the lack of outrage on the part of the majority of my fellow Americans, I can only guess that many do not understand either the humanity of children in the womb, nor the magnitude of the abortion tragedy. Every day between 3,000 and 4,000 children are killed through various abortion procedures. More children are killed every day through abortion than died during either the Pearl Harbor attack on December 7, 1941, or during the terrorist attacks on the World Trade Center on September 11, 2001. These two vile attacks, separated by 60 years, galvanized Americans to action, and resulted in the United States leading the fight that won World War II, and the dual victories over tyrannical regimes in Afghanistan and Iraq, respectively.

But despite the incredible number of innocent deaths, the American people have not risen up to stop abortion. In this 1st Pillar of Freedom I am calling for an end to this national tragedy, but I recognize that many of you have already been working toward this honorable goal for more than thirty years. It is my hope that the 1st Pillar of Freedom will add to the good work you are already doing!

Another way to understand the magnitude of abortion deaths in America is to realize that more children are killed every year in the womb than all the military deaths in our 228-year history. Though annual abortions have dropped in the US from approximately 1.6

million deaths in 1990, the total remains approximately 1.3 million per year.[1]

The Abortion Statistics component of the website just cited contains some interesting questions and answers, including the subject of why abortions are performed. The reason given by the overwhelming majority is sad: 95% of women have abortions as a means of birth control, while only 1% of abortions are performed because of rape or incest; 1% because of fetal abnormalities; and 3% because of the mother's health. Even if we accepted the necessity of the 5% of abortions done for reasons other than birth control, eliminating this 95% would save more than one million lives annually.

It is important to note here that modern medical technology and expertise can save most mothers and children in crises pregnancies, even where there is risk of death and serious injury. After these babies are born, if the mother/husband/family does not want to (or is not able to) raise their child, loving adoptive parents are available, and long to bring these children into their homes. And since in 97% of all pregnancies both mother and child are healthy, adoption will save unwanted children from certain death.

So why is there such ambivalence regarding abortion? I think that there are several reasons. First, there is a general lack of understanding that children's lives begin when the fertilized egg implants in the mother's uterus. Certainly the Roe v. Wade decision reflected this lack of understanding, where even our Supreme Court considered it appropriate to assign a constitutional 'right of privacy' to cases including a mother's right to kill her unborn child. It seems absurd that our Founders would support killing over one million healthy children annually in the name of privacy.

Second, the fetal life of every child is still more of a mystery to the general population than it should be, with many people ignorant of the fact that two and a half weeks after the egg's implantation his or her heart begins beating. Within those few short days, the transformation from a single-cell being to a complicated human embryo has progressed rapidly toward the recognizable child that will be born in a mere eight plus months. "All that is Added to the new human life from the moment of fertilization is time and nourishment...as for any growing child, teen, or adult."[2]

In only a few days, the tiny human progresses quickly from fertilized egg to fully recognizable baby in the womb. The genetic code is completely present at conception and is unique to that new person. At 18 days the heart begins to beat, and the baby's eyes begin developing on the 19th day. The baby's arms and legs begin developing at 4 weeks, and his or her mouth, ears, and nose begin taking shape. Brain waves are measurable at 6 weeks, as are kicking movements. By 8 weeks all the baby's systems are present and he or she can feel pain, and many babies begin sucking their thumbs. By 10 weeks the baby's body is completely formed, including fingerprints and eyelashes. Before the first trimester is completed, he or she is breathing (fluid), swallowing, digesting, sleeping, dreaming, waking, tasting, hearing, and learning. *"From this point on, the baby grows only in size."*[3]

The Center for Reclaiming America[4] has extracted some interesting quotes regarding verification of the humanity of the unborn child:

"Science is in Agreement: *It's a Human Life*

Physicians, biologists, and other scientists agree that conception (they define fertilization and conception to be the same) marks the beginning of a human being—a being that is alive and is a member of the human species. There is overwhelming agreement on this point in countless medical, biological, and scientific writings."
—Report, Subcommittee on Separation of Powers to Senate Judiciary Committee S-158, 97 Congress, 1st Session 1981, p.7.

"Pro-Abortionists Agree: *It's a Human Life*

Abortion Provider Admits that Abortion Kills Babies:

In 1965: 'an abortion kills the life of a baby after it has begun. It is dangerous to your life and health. It may make you sterile, so that when you want a child you cannot have it.'
Planned Parenthood, *Plan Your Children for Health and Happiness*, 1965.

In 1989: 'Women are not stupid...women have always known that there was a life there.'

Faye Wattleton past president of Planned Parenthood, NBC television broadcast, May 15, 1989.[5]

"The Founding Fathers Agree: *It's a Human Life*

'The care of human life and happiness and not their destruction is the first and only legitimate object of good government.'
—Thomas Jefferson

'We hold these truths to be self-evident, that all men are created equal, that they are endowed by their Creator with certain unalienable Rights, that among these are Life, Liberty and the pursuit of Happiness. That to secure these rights, Governments are instituted...'
—The Declaration of Independence

'...Nor shall any state deprive any person of life, liberty or property, without due process of law.'
—Amendment XIV, U.S. Constitution"

Additionally, the Reclaiming America website offers two quotes from notable 20th Century leaders:

"We hear the familiar cry that morals can't be legislated. This may be true, but behavior can be regulated. The law may not be able to make a man love me, but it can keep him from lynching me."
—Dr. Martin Luther King, Jr. [6]

"The so-called right to abortion has pitted mothers against their children and women against men. It has sown violence and discord at the heart of the most intimate human relationships.

It has aggravated the derogation of the father's role in an increasingly fatherless society. It has portrayed the greatest of gifts—a child—as a competitor, an intrusion, and an inconvenience."
—Mother Teresa [7]

It is universally agreed that approximately 97% of all pregnancies are normal — meaning that both mother and child are healthy. I confirmed this during my contemporary research and during conversations with a variety of medical doctors over many years. There is just an objective fact that everyone must face: "once a woman is pregnant, she already has a child; the choice is what to do with him or her. Although the word 'choice' sounds so positive, the actual choice is whether to have a live child or a dead child."[8]

Based on the foregoing, I advocate changing relevant laws here in America (and in as much of the rest of the world as we and other pro-life nations can influence) to protect all medically viable children from being killed by abortion. In the United States we should back this protection for the child from implantation to birth with a constitutional amendment. "Abortion" will only be permitted in medical emergencies. I place the word in quotes because I would not term the procedures described as abortions.

Is an abortion ever necessary?

The answer is no, not ever — the following situations will explain why.

There are times when a child is conceived in the mother's fallopian tubes instead of in the womb. This is called an ectopic pregnancy. Unless the embryonic child is removed from the tube, he or she will increase in size until the tube bursts, killing both mother and child. There is nothing that can presently be done to prevent this rare event from happening, and some type of surgery to remove the baby is the only option for saving the mother's life.

This is a situation where the baby will die anyway. Perhaps someday there will be a procedure to transfer the child to the womb, but that is not yet possible. The result of this procedure is a mother who survives and a baby who dies — but neither medical doctors nor I call this procedure an abortion.

Additional emergencies

There are other medical emergencies that affect both the mother and the baby in the womb, some of which, if not properly treated, will kill both. But these unusual situations must be considered in the context of the vast number of normal pregnancies and deliveries. When a mother is in the care of a physician in a modern hospital, maternal death is extremely rare. In one study, "over a decade, three major hospitals...report the delivery of 223,000 babies with only two maternal deaths, deaths that abortion would not have prevented."[9]

But tragically, there are cases where women have been in automobile or other accidents and are rushed to emergency rooms with life-threatening injuries. In these cases, caring for the mother is the primary concern of the medical team—particularly when they do not even know she is pregnant. When they discover she is pregnant they will try to save the life of the baby in the womb if possible, but if the woman's life is not saved, and the child has not reached the age of viability (meaning that he or she can live outside the mother), both will die anyway. These are terrible situations, but the kind that face medical professionals in emergency situations everyday. And we should thank God for those gifted by Him to be doctors and nurses!

The key point in these cases is that the mother's life-threatening situation is not a result of the pregnancy, but of an accident. And, equally important, it is not the intent of the medical team to kill the child, but to save both mother and child if possible.

Viability

It is my philosophical position that one innocent death is better than two, and I support procedures that save the most viable life, whether it is the mother's or the child's.

When referring to a child, I use the term viability to mean the ability of the child to live apart from the mother. In general, children can live outside the womb (with reasonable life-sustaining feeding and breathing assistance as is commonly provided in western hospitals) once they complete the 6th month of gestational life. Before that, babies are generally not formed enough to survive.

If the child has reached viability, I emphasize focusing on saving the child first. In fact, delivering the child will enhance treatment options for the mother, who is now able to receive care without regard to the child. If the mother is conscious, she (and the father if he is present) will know the baby is safe, relieving her and the family of mental anguish so she can receive life-saving medical treatments with peace of mind. The best of all outcomes is for both mother and child to survive, but where laws respect the child's viability, at least he or she will be saved.

However, there are times when the child is too young to survive outside the mother. In these sad cases, the medical team just has to do the best it can, and try to save the mother regardless of what happens to the child. The baby may have been injured in the accident, or will be killed during the mother's life-saving treatment. But again, the baby dies as a result of the accident or disease, or from treating the mother, not because it is the intent of either the mother or medical professionals to harm the child.

Early delivery

There are other situations that require "emergency premature delivery". Dr. Willke mentions two additional cases where children must be delivered early. The first is *toxemia*, and the second is *severe diabetic crises*.

In these cases, if the baby is not delivered prematurely, the mother will die, killing the child as well. But fortunately, both these conditions occur in the final trimester of the pregnancy, when most children have reached viability and can live outside the womb. Current medical technology allows these children to be delivered early so the mother can receive appropriate, life-saving treatment. The happy result is that both mother and child survive.

The bottom line in these cases is that they are not abortions. Though the children die in some cases, no one intends to kill the child.

Stem cells

As our medical/scientific capacities increase, we will have ethical challenges that match these advances. In one field of medical/cellular research, scientists have discovered that stem cells have remarkable properties for medical advancement and treatment of various conditions. But new ethical questions center on the source of the stem cells and the manner of their extraction.

The Bedford Research Foundation provides a useful definition of stem cells: "stem cells are the reserve supply of replacement cells that multiply when needed for repair. Some, but not all, organs and tissues in the body have a supply of stem cells that respond to damage. Skin is an example. Skin wounds are repaired by skin stem cells, liver damage is repaired by liver stem cells."[10]

Newly formed human embryos also contain stem cells. Some researchers advocate extracting them from the developing baby and using them in their experiments and related work. The problem is that the process of harvesting the cells kills the embryonic child. Though this seems a clear case of killing a human being, there are many that fall back on the position that a baby is not human until it is born—the same rationale that allows some to justify abortion at any stage of a human baby's development, up to and including killing the child during delivery (if any part of the baby's body is still in the mother, it is considered a medical situation wherein it is still legal to kill the child).

It is also incredibly hypocritical to allow partial birth abortion, when other laws protect children in the womb. For instance, it is a double murder if you intentionally kill a pregnant woman and her unborn child dies as well.

Since I take the position that life begins at implantation, I advocate laws that protect the child from that point onward. Comprehensive legal protection is necessary to protect the developing child from "means-justifying-the-ends" arguments that promote killing an embryo. This new law would restrict the creation of fertilized eggs to the creation of a child—regardless of whether conception occurred inside or outside of the womb. There is no justification for killing the most vulnerable in our society (developing in normal, sequential biological stages through which all of us must pass before birth). It is unjustifiable to kill a child to prolong an adult's mental or physical health.

I support active and innovative medical science that uses non-human embryos, adult human stem cells, or stem cells from cord blood, for research and procedures. But extracting these cells does not kill the donor.[11]

Partial birth abortion

Believe it or not, before a law was passed in 2003 and upheld by the US Supreme Court, it was legal to kill a child before he or she was fully out of the mother's birth canal. The details of this procedure are too ghastly to recount here, but if you want to read a description please go to the Life Issues website.[12]

Popular talk show host Sean Hannity recounts an interview with Patricia Ireland (president of the National Organization for Women) in which he asked her to admit that killing a child during the gruesome partial birth abortion procedure was wrong, but she chose to speak only about the life of the mother. He commented as he interviewed her that "the American Medical Association supported the ban on partial birth abortion and that former surgeon general C. Everett Koop had explained that, with all that modern medicine has to offer, partial birth abortion is never needed to save the life or health of the mother. There are other ways to care for the woman."[13]

I hate to even mention this next gruesome topic, but the question of what sometimes happens to the bodies of aborted children is valid. Some years ago a garbage truck pulled up to the back of an abortion clinic to pick up the weekly trash. Inside a dumpster the G-men discovered a large number of aborted children's bodies, and these decent men refused to treat the deceased children as refuse. Following some legal wrangling in which pro-life supporters requested the right to bury the children properly, the fetal children were given a decent burial in a local cemetery.

But even more disturbing is evidence that some aborted children's bodies are dismembered so the parts can be sold, either through quasi-legal or illegal channels for transplantation or research purposes. For more facts pertaining to this highly disturbing issue, please see the Life News website.[14]

Rape and Incest

Rape is one of the worst violations that one human being can force on another, but in some cases, a baby is conceived as a result of this violent act. A serious ethical question facing society regarding such children is, in its righteous anger to bring the rapist to justice, should society permit violence against the innocent child?

This is not an easy question, but, because it is a life and death issue, one that deserves a clear set of laws. I would like to discuss the abortion aspect of this issue here, and save the crime and punishment aspect of rape and incest for the 2nd Pillar (reforming our legal code).

In some rape cases, the women is so badly injured that it is impossible to save a child conceived by the assault. In fact, the blood tests revealing pregnancy may not even be ordered by the physician during the patient's life-saving medical procedures or subsequent hospital stay. X-rays, surgery and other treatments may be necessary to save the mother from death. In these tragic cases, the baby in its early embryonic stage will die, but it is not the intent of either mother or medical professional to kill the child.

But there are other cases of rape, where the mother's injuries are not life threatening, and after she heals from the physical aspects of the attack she discovers she is pregnant. Now we have a different situation—a live and healthy baby and a traumatized mother. I advocate extending the laws of protection to such children, but also being fully supportive if the mother wishes to give the baby up for adoption after her son or daughter is born.

I would apply these same principles to incest victims, and any children so-conceived. In cases where the pregnant woman is a minor, she should be removed from the dangerous and dysfunctional situation and placed in a caring, protective environment. After the mother gives birth, the child may then be given up for adoption.

World population

There was a time when some of those concerned with world population advocated abortion as a necessary component of limiting the number of humans. They were afraid we'd overrun our planet and eat ourselves out of house and home. Though I favor good stewardship—that is, taking care of our entrusted resources and only having as many children as we can properly care for—I am completely against killing children as a means of controlling world population.

However, it is important to note that overpopulation in most of the world is a myth, and that we must now be concerned about the opposite problem. Unfortunately for our survival as a species, the real problem facing the world, particularly the developed world, is under-population—we are a dying race.

For example, the fertility rate in Russia is so bad that their population is predicted to decline from its current (2004) total of 148 million, to only 58 million by 2040—just 36 years from now! Similar trends have been discovered in Japan and Western Europe where the graying of the population is creating a crisis of caring for the elderly.

There are simply not enough younger people coming along to provide for their elders. China too is facing a severe aging crisis, and the abortion catastrophe there has added to imbalances (discussed below) that are extraordinary.

In the United States, we are barely holding our own with a birth-rate of 2.1%, just enough to maintain our replacement rate. But as discussed in the demographic projection section of the 4th Pillar, we also face a severe imbalance of elderly to young people in the next quarter century.

Only in some underdeveloped countries is the birthrate high enough to maintain growth—or in some cases to remain a problem.

This declining birthrate crisis is caused by a number of factors, but one of the most significant is abortion: There is an entire generation of children missing in the US: between 40 and 50 million children have been killed through abortion in the last 30 years, and worldwide, the number of abortions is staggering. Approximately 46 million fetal children are killed annually (about 126,000 per day), meaning that every year, the number of children aborted approximates the total number of people killed in WWII, to date the most destructive war in history.[15]

In China the problem is so bad (because of the selective killing of baby girls in the womb or later as infants and toddlers) that there is a shortage of eligible young women available for marriage. The abortion rate in China is more than double ours, and they have five times the population. These two figures alone help us conservatively calculate the number of abortions in China annually at more than 10 million.

Kotlikoff and Burns comment on this imbalance of eligible women to men: "China's population will be profoundly unbalanced because males will continue to outnumber females at all ages through the early 60's. Referred to as the 'missing girls problem,' the imbalance has its roots in a long-standing cultural preference for male children, a preference that was exacerbated by a government edict limiting the number of children a woman could have. Today, males age 15 to 59 outnumber females in the same age range by 25.4 million. By 2025 the mismatch will reach 30.7 million, 31.3 million by 2050."[16]

So how do we stop the abortion epidemic?

Here in the United States, where the practice of abortion is a continuing indictment against our idealism and heritage, the people have to rise up and say, enough! Even if all the gray areas are exempted from the discussion of necessity, more than 1 million children are unnecessarily killed every year in our nation founded on "life, liberty, and the pursuit of happiness".

In the 1st Pillar of Freedom I advocate passing a comprehensive law forbidding abortion at any time from implantation through delivery, excepting only the type of true medical emergencies described above. These (fortunately rare) situations are not abortions, but are rather the side affects of trying to save a mother's life in a life-threatening crisis.

Of great blessing, however, is the fact that children can now be safely delivered in the later stages of development, and live normal lives with only a simple boost from modern medical technology. Once babies can breathe on their own and nurse normally, they can come home from the hospital to loving families (natural or adoptive) and lead full, normal and happy lives.

Besides establishing a new legal standard that protects children in the womb, an amendment to our constitution is necessary to add additional protection and permanence to the new law. Such an amendment would make it much more difficult for future generations to ever again practice this objective evil.

Stopping abortion is the goal of the 1st Pillar of Freedom.

Notes

(1) For an overview of US and worldwide abortion statistics, please see www.abortiontv.com/ AbortionStatistics.htm)

(2) *Abortion on demand in America*, Fastfacts, The Center for Reclaiming America, www.reclaiming america.org. Page 2.

(3) Ibid.

(4) www.reclaimingamerica.org, page 1.

(5) During my sixteen years in professional ministry (eight full time, eight part-time, with fourteen of the sixteen years an army chaplain) I had the privilege of counseling a few women who were requesting prayer for healing from post-abortion trauma—and for God's mercy to help them conceive again. In most cases they had been single when they had the abortion and didn't want the child at the time. I never met a woman that looked back on her abortion as a good thing, or something she would do again now that she had either become a Christian, or become serious about her religious faith.

I also believe I saved at least one life by encouraging a courageous woman who decided to endure whatever ridicule she had to endure from her fellow soldiers and others, in order to bring her baby to term and give him or her up for adoption. She decided against having an abortion after agreeing to a referral to a local civilian crises pregnancy center where they lovingly showed her illustrations of what her unborn child looked like in the womb. Somewhere in the world is one human being I had a small part in saving. Today, ultrasound technology all women to view their fetal children in real time. I am an ultrasound tech and it is wonderful to see mother's and families reactions to their newest (in-utero) family member!

(6) www.reclaimingamerica.org, page 1.

(7) Ibid, page 2.

(8) Ibid.

(9) Dr. J. C. Willke, Life Issues Connector: July 2000, page 1. Please see their website at: www.lifeissues.org/connector/00 jul.html

(10) Please see the Bedford Research Foundation's website at www. bedfordresearch.org/stemcell/stemcell.php?item=stemcell_ faqs, page 1. This four-page website answers many questions on stem cell research and cloning, and explains some of the moral and ethic problems inherent in related research.

(11) For a heart-warming testimony regarding adult donation of stem cells, please see the Family Research Council's Center for Human Life and Bioethics website:

www.frc.org/get.cfm?i=NW04B34, then follow the prompts to www.frc.org/get.cfm?i= PV04G02&f=HB04B01. The article is by cancer survivor, Miss Sara Rudolph.

Also on the FRC's website is a related article regarding the successful implanting of 12 year-old embryos in a mother which produced twins, and comments on the Italian fertility law that prohibits more than 3 embryos being created outside the womb at one time. A provision of this law requires that all three embryonic children must be implanted in the mother. This testimony supports the obvious humanity and healthy potential of all fertilized human eggs, and is a model law protecting all children from the moment of conception through birth.

(12) www.lifeissues.org/connector/00jul.html, pages 7-8.

(13) Sean Hannity, *Let Freedom Ring; Winning the War of Liberty over Liberalism*, Regan Books, 2002, page 182. This is a must read! Obviously our society has a ways to go in our ethics—I hope that the 1st Pillar of Freedom contributes to our national repentance and healing.

(14) www.lifenews.com. Follow the various discussions of the ethics and morality of trafficking in baby body parts. It is a subject that is starting to catch the media's attention.

(15) www.abortiontv.com/AbortionStatistics.htm, page 4.

(16) Laurence J. Kotlikoff and Scott Burns, *The Coming Generational Storm: What You Need to Know about America's Economic Future*. The MIT Press, Cambridge, Massachusetts, 2004, page 38.

"Do not be overcome by evil, but overcome evil with good."
Romans 12:21 (NIV)

"Everyone must submit himself to the governing authorities, for there is no authority except that which God has established. The authorities that exist have been established by God. Consequently, he who rebels against the authority is rebelling against what God has instituted, and those who do so will bring judgment on themselves. For rulers hold no terror for those who do right, but for those who do wrong…if you do wrong, be afraid, for he does not bear the sword for nothing. He is God's servant, an agent of wrath to bring punishment on the wrongdoer."
Romans 13:1-4 (NIV)

CHAPTER TWO

The 2nd Pillar of Freedom: Legal Reforms

Introduction

O ur current legal system is one of the best in the world — indeed, I would not want to live under any other. But that said, America is awash in crime, and though trends are improving, there is no reason why our citizens must tolerate this solvable problem. Our minimal expectation should be to live our daily lives without fear of predatory criminals. The goal of the 2nd Pillar is to eliminate crime or criminals — their choice.

Let's be frank, there are violent people scattered throughout our society, criminals who prey upon the innocent, committing crimes of every kind. Things are so bad that about one percent of our population is in jail — a shocking figure in a democracy such as ours. They rob and rape, kill and destroy, cheat on their taxes and cook their books, and law-abiding citizens want it stopped.

In the 2nd Pillar of Freedom I recommend changes to our legal system that will significantly reduce crime. These changes emphasize adopting new and harsher penalties for all crimes — each designed to frighten criminals into abandoning their plans before they carry them out. These new laws are intended to prevent both initial crimes and recidivism.

On the other hand, unnecessary lawsuits are suffocating our legal system. When our judges and courts are freed from unnecessary work, everyone will benefit. The entire system will be more efficient and better able to exonerate the innocent, prosecute and punish the guilty, and give everyone greater confidence in our democracy.

Background

Our society is overly litigious and lawsuits are running amok. The current legal system allows frivolous lawsuits that are totally without legal merit. These swamp our congested and overburdened courts, judges, juries, and jails. The system also allows ridiculous monetary awards that drain societies' resources and inflate the prices of everything we purchase. Hidden legal costs are pervasive, and along with the allied requirement to over-insure against liability, are built into every price structure.

We are so litigious that business initiatives are often viewed as too risky. Medical malpractice is driving wonderfully trained physicians away from medicine, or forcing them to pay for exorbitant insurance. These costs are then passed along to consumers, driving the costs of health care to artificially inflated levels. The legal aspects of health care reform will be presented in the 6th Pillar.

This negative and inefficient legal environment has caused neighbors to hesitate before helping each other—even to the point of not wanting to watch each other's children. We hesitate to provide traditional 'good Samaritan' acts of kindness and mercy. We also hesitate to become teachers because unruly students know they can get away with almost anything, and teachers in certain situations even fear for their physical safety on school grounds. We hesitate to discipline our children for fear that a nosey neighbor might call the police and accuse us of child abuse—resulting in our being watched by "big brother" for years.

2nd Pillar changes will eliminate most of these problems, and will prevent crime and help law-abiding citizens to have more confidence as they live in and serve our society.

Mutual responsibility in our law-abiding society

We are a nation of interdependent citizens. If we were not, if ultimately we were strictly a nation of individuals, without allegiance to church, nation, family or neighbors; if we had no societal responsibilities; if we were a nation of proverbial islands with no primary responsibilities to one another, then we could live in a hedonistic fog of drug-induced irresponsibility.

But that is not the basis of American life. We are a people whose founders and ancestors risked everything to build a society based on Biblical principles that were later incorporated into our Constitution, a comprehensive legal document delineating sacrificial interdependence.

Our democracy thrives by balancing the needs and desires of both the individual and the group. In that vital sense, hedonism or even radical libertarianism can damage our society. We are an independent people, yet who are highly dependent on each other. We have laws is because we have always chosen to be an organized society rather than a chaotic one. We naturally gravitate towards organization because it is programmed into us by the Master Organizer. Sin breeds the chaotic side of our nature.

I am reasonably libertarian—particularly when its philosophy of individual liberty and responsibility is applied to economics. But any individual freedom, whether it pertains to ingesting dangerous drugs, or using caustic chemicals, machinery, or firearms, must be balanced with individual responsibility and accountability to our greater society. The needs of our fellow citizens also matter, and self-destructive behaviors often hurt others. We place limits on our freedoms for practical reasons, and in our representative, republican form of government, our laws are established after debates, discussion, and ultimately legislative action. Judges who act above the law or who create laws on their own are rebelling against the Constitution.

Having standards is part of our system, as is deciding together what these standards should be. By working through the legal process, 'We the People' can set the bar wherever we want. Our lawmakers, elected within the framework of our republican form of government, act on societies' behalf. Ultimately, however, it is the citizens who determine our laws—with our beliefs, our history, and our Constitution as our guide.

Examples

Consider driving. All states assert that driving is a privilege with attendant responsibilities. The reasons for this are simple — driving without qualifications or in violation of the law can be lethal. In this regard, the licensing process can be a life or death issue.

The same is true of medicines (and illegal drugs) that can ruin your mind and body if taken improperly. When you destroy yourself (slowly or quickly), you deny your fellow citizens the contributions you could have made to society, and if your altered state makes you a dangerous person, you can hurt others.

Handling dangerous chemicals or firearms in an irresponsible manner can injure or kill your fellow citizens. Mutual responsibility (even in the context of strong support for Second Amendment rights to bear arms) is the bottom line in any organized society—a principle also taught in the Bible and in our Constitution.

Firearms are a major issue these days. Our founders fought for our independence and established our republic by bearing arms in defense of the new nation. National defense was conducted in the context of a heavily armed foreign state forcing its will on our ancestors via an oppressive colonial government that denied them equal representation under British law.

This first generation of American patriots initially appealed to the British government for proper treatment, but after being repeatedly rebuffed, declared their independence. The British response was to send a large professional army from Europe to invade our fledgling democracy—trying to force its will upon a people wanting freedom. The patriots countered this foreign threat by organizing militias comprised of armed citizens who brought their individual weapons to battle.

But the other context of the Second Amendment is the right to bear arms to protect oneself and one's family and neighbors—not just to defend the country against foreign attack. Patriots drew heavily on their Christian worldview of individual responsibility, and applied this philosophy in this fallen and dangerous world. Bearing arms in the early days of our existence—from pilgrim days onward—was key to self-defense in the absence of military or police protection.

And this principle of self-protection is still valid and vital today: everyone is obligated to protect themselves and their families from criminal aggression until the police arrive. Whether we are residents of modern cities or ranchers living in the remotest parts of America, owning and using personal firearms responsibly is a key to survival during that life and death gap—that time from the moment of the first criminal threat until the time the police arrive. And the more rural the residence or the more occupied the police force (perhaps during a larger crises such as a natural disaster or civil disturbance) the longer the time gap before the police arrive.

The dangers of our pioneer years have passed, but our current society if full of dangerous criminals, and we have a Constitutional responsibility to protect our families from evil—certainly until our outstanding professional police forces can arrive on the scene.

Unless we as a society decide to assign a policeman to guard every small business or home, there will always be this protection gap. In those critical minutes, possession of a firearm can mean the difference between life and death. Conversely, it is logical that criminals want an unarmed citizenry that is easy to prey upon.

There are those (probably well meaning pacifists) that advocate disarming the American people—taking guns from everyone except government entities of various kinds. But how often in history has a government been able to abolish criminal intent? Even when punishments are increased to curtail crime, there will always be a bold criminal element that will foolishly risk all in the pursuit of evil. I share the often-stated belief that when it becomes a crime for ordinary citizens to own guns, only criminals and the government officials will have guns—and the people will be defenseless against both. Neither the illegal criminal element, nor our neighbors whom we elect to govern us, should have all the power.

We tend to trust our government, and that is good, but we should never abrogate our ultimate responsibility to defend ourselves. Our brave police forces and National Guard troops are there to assist us as we defend ourselves—but we should never be naive enough to leave ourselves defenseless in a hostile world. In our society, the individual is always the ultimate check and balance against evil. And on a lighter side, when asked if I support gun control I usually say yes...always use two hands!

The balanced role of government

That said, our neighbors whom we elect to govern us do have a responsibility, even in the context of the Second Amendment, to place restrictions on the ownership and use of firearms. I advocate placing reasonable limits on firearm ownership and use—a balanced democratic approach that considers both the needs of the individual and the needs of our greater society. All responsible adult citizens have the right to bear arms, as the Constitution makes clear, but it also includes principles that can be applied to determine how much freedom individual gun owners have. The line will be drawn at a place that the two parties (individual gun owners and our greater society) can live with—no pun intended.

Most adults have the right in our system to own a gun, but I advocate granting a permit to carry a firearm only to those trained to use one. Every adult who desires to carry a firearm should be able to apply to their local police department for a permit, and should be granted a license after passing reasonably priced policesponsored (or equivalent) training and testing that the applicant pays for. Persons with mental illness or violent criminal backgrounds should be prohibited from obtaining permits or from purchasing or owning firearms. There should be no registration of firearms, but requiring a short waiting period to evaluate an applicant or purchaser's record is acceptable. This balancing of freedom and responsibility will greatly deter crime, be of great benefit to our police forces, and help us remain safe and free.

Illegal drugs

Drug use is a significant problem in our society and I offer here a reasonable set of solutions. First, in light of the philosophy of mutual responsibility discussed above, I am against lifting prohibitions against illegal drugs. But, at the same time, I do want to empty our prisons of drug users—time spent in the current prison system being generally a large waste of time and treasure for all concerned.

In place of incarceration for illegal drug use (in the context of individual use that did not include a larger crime such as driving under the influence, etc., especially if someone else was harmed), I advocate a regimen of counseling, combined with mandatory restitution for the costs of police, court, and counseling programs. Counselors will be assigned by the presiding judge, and may be secular or religious, doctors or pastors—whomever has basic training in assisting addicts to transition to a healthy lifestyle.

As long as the offence is illegal substance use alone, counseling seems to me to be the best corrective action, even for repeat offenders. Counseling costs will be paid for by the offender—in immediate cash or working off the costs through public service.

For all higher levels of illegal drug activity, including manufacture, sale, or distribution, the escalating punishments outlined below are appropriate—and will significantly deter drug use as well.

Punishing criminals in a just society

I recommend that all criminals be judged and punished according to the first crime they commit under the new system—a system with penalties harsh enough that even advertising them will deter crime. These changes will also end most recidivism.

First of all, I recommend changing the way accused persons are treated during the initial phase of their confrontation with the legal system. A judge in a closed courtroom should examine all relevant facts to determine if the case has sufficient merit to proceed to the next step. Judges will refer medical cases to the new medical court system, which specializes in medical malpractice cases. This new parallel court system is presented in the 6th Pillar.

All accused persons will be afforded strict rights in accordance with our long-standing American principle that a person is innocent until proven guilty. However, obviously violent offenders, or persons that are deemed by the judge to be flight risks in capital cases, may be held pending the outcome of their case and/or a change in their status. Therefore, excepting the police and district attorney's investigation, I advocate complete protection of the identity of the accused except as is necessary for the collection of evidence to either convict or exonerate them. If the accused chooses to reject this protective measure, he or she should have full rights to do so.

If the judge believes there is sufficient evidence for the person to be tried for the crime, then the accused will be tried according to current law. When the trial is completed, the accused will be acquitted or sentenced, then freed or punished as directed by the judge using the new guidelines recommended in this chapter.

Professional jurors

I recommend that we abandon our current practice of using untrained regular citizens as jurors, and transition to a new system utilizing trained professionals. Though our current system is part of our tradition and appeals to our sense of public service, having professional jurors will increase the likelihood that justice will be dispensed more objectively and accurately. An additional benefit is that private citizens will no longer have their lives disrupted— where hundreds of people are screened for the few unbiased slots required for a jury seating.

Accuser responsibility

Another recommend change regards the accuser. In the course of the initial judicial screening, follow-on investigation and trial, the charges against the defendant will be examined to determine guilt or innocence. In the case of insufficient evidence and acquittal, the accused will be released without penalty. But what happens to the person who filed the complaint? I recommend that in cases where the accuser is proven to have intentionally lied and brought false charges against the defendant, that he or she be given the same punishment that the falsely accused defendant would have received had they bee proven guilty.

This modification alone will greatly reduce the caseloads currently overwhelming our legal system, and should nearly eliminate false accusations. In cases where the defendant is proven guilty, I recommend the following punishments.

The Death Penalty

I am in favor of the death penalty for all heinous crimes. It is a just end for criminals guilty of capital crimes and an effective deterrent to others considering such crimes. This punishment should be reserved for adults and older teens tried as adults.

When the state executes a person who commits a brutal crime, it acts as an instrument of society, administering justice rather than meting out personal revenge. Legal execution ends the cycle of violence, whereas an inadequate punishment system promotes individual or mob revenge, thus promoting further violence. If the state fails to carry out its responsibility, it only encourages the aggrieved parties to take matters into their own hands.

The state must carry out executions after due process, and kill the guilty party in a quick and humanitarian way. But the state must also execute those who deserve this punishment in a timely fashion, and the appellate process should not be allowed to drag on for years. I recommend that the appellate process be limited to not more than six months following initial conviction. Governors should retain the right to offer one brief stay of execution where circumstances dictate, but only the president should have clemency power.

Crimes deserving this ultimate penalty should include murder *and attempted murder*, capital rape (cases where the victim is violently beaten in additional to being subjected to the heinous violation of rape, plus cases where the victim is a young minor under fourteen and the criminal is at least twenty-one). Also included should be any crime where the victim is killed during an assault or robbery, or where firearms are used in the crime—even if the firearms are not discharged; treason, kidnapping, manufacturing, distributing, or selling significant amounts of illegal drugs, *and for repeated crimes of the next lower level of severity.*

Exceptional Cases

In cases where a severe crime is committed by a severely mentally handicapped person, a more appropriate punishment may be a life sentence in a mental facility for the criminally insane. However, the presiding judge must insure that the guilty party is not using the insanity plea as a dodge. Three licensed psychiatrists should be employed to make an insanity evaluation.

In cases where the criminal is very young (in our modern society this probably means a young teen or pre-teen), they may be shown some leniency for a first offence and given a strict regime of punishment that may include counseling or a "boot camp" type of incarceration deemed appropriate by the court. Youth in this category should not be released back into society until they are proven to be responsible [perhaps after their term of mandatory national service (from ages eighteen to twenty) when they could prove their trustworthiness].

Social crimes such as prostitution should be treated with counseling after the first conviction. Both parties should receive the same punishment. A second conviction by either party should result in dramatically increased fines and/or public restitution.

Prisoners and Prisons

I advocate changing our policies regarding prisoners and prisons. The emphasis in dealing with all criminals who have committed white collar or non-violent (or mildly violent behavior) should shift from punishing them with incarceration to exacting restitution. Unless the prison is specifically constructed and run as a productive factory that produces something useful to taxpayers and where the criminal can earn enough money to pay his or her restitution, such prison time is wasted time, removing from society the productivity and restitution that a victim or society should expect from the criminal. However those criminals convicted of major white-collar and other medium-level crimes should receive heavy fines in addition to their restitution requirement.

Prisons not specifically geared to factory/farm operations should either be closed or transformed into prisoner holding and processing facilities only—preparing prisoners for an assigned term of productive work somewhere appropriate. Prisoners should be severely warned that prison time is an opportunity to make restitution, and that non-cooperation or escape will yield quick escalation to the next higher category of punishment.

Those prisoners trying to escape would receive additional confinement for a first offense, and the death penalty for a second offense (providing they were adults). This type of escalating punishment will end recidivism.

During the new prisoner's induction phase, he or she should be evaluated for gifts and talents and assigned appropriate work accordingly—either inside the factory prison or in a more useful place. Perhaps prisoner battalions could assist in government infrastructure construction projects.

Whatever the circumstance, until their release, prisoners must be treated humanely, but will do what they are told, when they are told to do it. When their debt to society has been paid in full, they will be released with the hope that they will never again commit any crime, and with a stern warning regarding the next level of punishment if they do.

When the restitution/incarceration term is completed, prisoners will be returned to the prison for out-processing and released back into society.

Policy Summary

Crime flourishes where it is tolerated, and I believe that appropriately severe punishment deters crime. Though criminals often do stupid things, all people are inherently interested in self-preservation. Therefore I advocate changing our legal system so that potential criminals are intimidated by severe penalties into forgoing crime.

There is no need for law-abiding citizens to endure abuse, and no excuse for criminals to prey upon our society. Those that do so must be severely punished or eliminated. Their choice.

"I looked and saw all the oppression that was taking
place under the sun: I saw the tears of the oppressed—and they
have no comforter; power was on the side of their oppressors—and
they have no comforter. And I declared that the dead, who had
already died, are happier than the living, who are still alive. But
better than both is he who…has not seen the evil
that is done under the sun."
Ecclesiastes 4:1-3 (NIV)

CHAPTER THREE

The 3rd Pillar of Freedom: National Security and International Relations

Introduction

Americans have a clear choice: either we can try to hunker down behind our protective oceans or we can engage the world. Either we believe that the world will be safer if we stay here and rely on the United Nations and hope for the best, or we can commit ourselves to positive unilateralism and protect our friends and interests worldwide, and rid the world of dictators and thugs and free most of the world from their tyranny. 9/11 proved there is no middle ground.

There are obvious limits to what any one nation can do (even the United States) but not doing what we can seriously destabilizes our world. Just as the obviously absent local policeman creates instability, so is the world less stable when America turns it focus inward. And make no mistake—the United States is the world's policeman—the only question is whether we are a responsibly pro-active policeman or an aloof one. By moving outward with clear purpose and good intent, and with the help of friends who choose to join us, we can eliminate most of the despots that still lurk in the underdeveloped world, thus freeing millions of suffering people.

My presupposition is that this world is fallen, and as the only friendly superpower, and without our positive intervention, it is a more dangerous and violent place. Therefore, non-interventionist philosophy, including appeasement in the face of aggressive bullies (whether a nation state or terrorist group), will only encourage the propagation of evil and needless death and suffering by innocent people. We must be a positive force for good on every continent or those committed to evil will win!

There are those Americans who hint at, or outright proclaim, that the "bad guys" attacked us here because we have been engaged "over there". But I believe the opposite: that we were attacked here because we are not engaged "over there" enough! Some even blame America for the evils of the terrorists, but that kind of thinking only aids and abets our enemies, giving them encouragement instead of proper condemnation.

Because I believe the world has many dangerous regimes and groups committed to our destruction and that of our friends, I recommend that the United States pro-actively seek out and eliminate any threat posed by terrorist groups or rogue regimes. Whether these evil entities threaten us, or more vulnerable people who need our help, we should intervene and eliminate evil—and stay as long as necessary until a reasonable stability is achieved.

The world also has a clear choice: those who want to be known as our friends will join us in this great task as best they can. Those political entities, which want to remain neutral (and are not using "neutrality" as a guise to oppress peaceful neighbors or innocent minorities within their own borders) can expect to be treated as such, and be limited in their trading opportunities in the greatest market on earth. But those regimes or groups that threaten us, or abuse the helpless (or facilitate those that do) should expect us to move swiftly to eliminate them and replace their objective evil with objective (democratic) good. At a minimum, bullying totalitarian regimes should be replaced with multi-party democracies, complete with constitutions that protect their people's basic freedoms—such as those enjoyed in much of the free world.

I am fully aware that I am proclaiming this policy not only to my fellow Americans, but also to our many international friends (and others who would like us to act more forthrightly so they can trust us enough to become our friends). Further, because this policy affects them as well, I am also indirectly addressing potential enemies wherever they might exist.

Since the 3rd Pillar effects so many, let me emphasize at the start that I advocate living in peace with everyone possible—enjoying mutually beneficial relations with every nation and culture on earth. And, as long as our citizens and friends benefit, American policies should be directed to that end. Every good we do should also be considered in light of our duty to protect our own interests—that is, making the world a safer place to live for all Americans.

America desires to be a useful ally among the family of nations. We have been given the diverse resources we enjoy (the most remarkable of which are our amazing citizens who have come here from every nation, culture, language group, and religion on earth) not only to rejoice in what we have, but also to be both an example of good stewardship and a pro-active servant-friend to everyone possible.

America has traveled a long and difficult road to get to the point where we are—the only superpower. Today, we are many generations removed from that fledgling republic that was, of necessity, inwardly focused. Our founders cautioned against external entanglements in those early days for the practical reason that we were fighting for our very survival. Also, it is debatable whether even the most visionary among our founders could have imagined what would happen to the new nation they were risking everything to create and fight for.

It took us many years to get our own house stabilized before we could accept the ever-growing international responsibilities that faced us in the nineteenth century—particularly during wars with Mexico and later Spain. But what is most important is that we **did** face our external threats, and after nearly four centuries of colonial and independent sojourn, we are still **the** lighthouse—**the** beacon of freedom that draws the world to our door.

Background

Circumstances early in the nineteenth century forced us to think internationally. We were invaded by Great Britain during the War of

1812, and before that we had to deal with the North African piracy crises during the First Barbary War (1801-1805), and periods of conflict continued in the region for decades.

Later, because of the Alamo and the unstable and threatening situation emanating from the growing conflict in Texas, we had our war with Mexico.

Next, in the middle of the nineteenth century, we had to pay an awful price for tolerating the national sin of slavery. We allowed human bondage to remain in post-colonial America, tolerating it even as we wrote the Constitution after winning our national freedom. It is my personal belief that God extracted the price of 600,000 American lives during the Civil War to test our viability as a future superpower. He does not tolerate a high level of sin forever, and at some point extracts a terrible price from the unrepentant.

Once we passed through that refining fire, we were able to move forward. Though vestiges of the old order remained via the racist Jim Crow laws and segregation, the country steadily addressed the issues of racism over the next century, a trend which culminated with passage of comprehensive civil rights legislation in the mid-1960's. This legislation finalized the related Constitutional Amendments passed earlier.

But by the end of the century we were strong enough, and established enough here at home, to consistently venture out from the relative safety of our shores. God protected us with those ocean barriers until we were strong enough to be useful.

During the long post-civil war transition, if we had remained inwardly focused after we had developed to the point where we could make a real difference outside of our boarders, we would have been selfish and properly open to criticism. But that said, we must admit that our forays into the international scene have not always been mutually beneficial. The development of our foreign policy has been a learning process, and from time to time we've made costly mistakes. Let us learn the appropriate lessons: we should not avoid engagement, but we should engage with overwhelming force and a systematic plan to rebuild the newly liberated nations as long-term friends—for mutually beneficial reasons.

Naiveté

We have no excuse for being surprised by evil in a fallen world, and naiveté, particularly regarding the immense and growing threat of radical Islam, is not only irresponsible, but will get Americans and others killed. If an entity is bent on destroying us, we'd better be proactive or we'll, ironically, just enable our own demise.

This latest chapter of American naiveté began during the 1970's with the Arab oil embargo in 1973—a situation followed by the debacle of the Iran hostage fiasco a few years later (1979-1981). If we had unilaterally and pro-actively dealt with those dire threats, we would have spared the world at least a portion of the continuing danger of radical Islam. We are still reaping the fruit of our failure to act. Terrorism is on the rise and Iran is developing its nuclear infrastructure and will shortly have the ability to build nuclear weapons.

Our bonehead policy towards Iran when the Shaw was deposed was just the latest in a series of international policy blunders that include ignoring the rapidly growing threat that fascism posed in the 1930's. Later we allowed the spread of nuclear weapons in the Soviet Union and China, and our hesitation in Korea allowed a divided peninsula and a nuclear North Korea now. We have reaped a much more dangerous world today by tolerating the spread of these three menaces (radical Islam, weapons of mass destruction, and adventurous dictators), and each of these strengthened because we **hoped** the world would be as good as we are. How many people have died, and how many more will die, because well meaning leaders either think the best of vicious foreign killers, or hide their heads in the sand?

Fortunately, our history is balanced with examples of bold leaders who directed well-coordinated military campaigns overseas, where we protected our interests and those of our friends, and came to the aid of violently oppressed minorities. We continued to engage (though often too slowly and too late) during the twentieth century, protecting our self-interest while defending Western Europe (twice) and the Pacific from fascist/imperial aggression. During these long and difficult decades we evolved into the leader of the free world that we are today—the principle country to whom oppressed people everywhere can turn for help.

Interventions in Korea, Vietnam, Nicaragua, Kuwait, Iraq, and Afghanistan solidified our expanding role as defender and liberator in a dangerous world, and proving that we are willing to proactively risk much and suffer much to assist our neighbors wherever they live. We learned lessons along the way—the most of which are to understand situations before they explode (utilizing improved intelligence collection and analysis), then to intervene before the situation develops to the point where tragedy overwhelms an opportunity for peace and/or a quick resolution to the looming conflict.

Appeasement has rightly become a dirty word in our international vocabulary, but we must guard ourselves from ever falling back into the old delusions that we can love or bribe evil into submission. I fully support and respect the sacrificial agape love of modern missionaries—those who risk their lives in desperate situations in service to God. But the national policy of America should stress peace through strength—and we must maintain enough military power to bring down threatening regimes efficiently.

Spiritually we should not rely on the numbers of our chariots or the power of our horses, but in this fallen world we must be as smart as foxes, and wise and powerful when dealing with ruthless enemies.

Currently it is in our mutual best interest to help Afghanistan and Iraq, and the world was able to see a modest yet tangible result of American unilateralism (which included several nations that joined us) when female athletes from these two formerly repressed nations were able to openly march and compete in the Athens Olympics. These two nations are in the early stages of a long-term transition from totalitarianism to reasonable democracy because of the proactive policies of President Bush. Recognized free governments lead both emerging democracies, and within a short time, free elections will solidify these new friends. What could be better than turning an enemy into a friend?

To be frank, if we had entered WWI sooner, and stayed to solidify a fairer peace, WWII could have been avoided. And please remember that World War II cost the lives of fifty million people, and untold amounts of other human suffering and expended treasure.

North Korea would not be the dangerous problem it is today if we'd invested more resources and satisfactorily completed the 1950-1953 Korean War. Instead of leaving behind a unified and democratic Korean Peninsula, we failed to complete the mission and now have to live with a dangerous rogue state with nuclear weapons. Additionally, we left behind an enslaved people—a portion of Asia that has been forced to live under a brutal and uncompromising successor dictatorship for more than half a century. This is the kind of disaster that a United Nations-led mission delivers. Only an American-led mission can fully accomplish the kind of lasting peace such as the world enjoys in Europe and Japan.

We made another mistake by supporting French recolonialization of Vietnam, rather than maintaining our support for the fledgling democracy we helped establish at end of World War II. In Vietnam our OSS commandos had been working with Vietnamese partisans to defeat the Japanese, and just at the critical juncture of history when a coalition of nationalists was establishing a postcolonial government with our help, our government abandoned this newly independent state by supporting British efforts to help France reestablish control over its colony.

If we had continued our support for the newly independent state of Vietnam, and assisted them as they transitioned into a fully functional, multi-party democracy and friend, we could have prevented the thirty-year tragedy that followed, and the one-party communist government that continues today. The death toll between 1945 and 1975 was staggering: some three million Vietnamese, ninety thousand French, and sixty thousand Americans and others were killed, plus an untold number wounded. Today the after-affects of that war still hurt all concerned. Sure, the French should rightly bear the lion's share of the blame for their terrible decision to reassert their claim to a former colony (and the British bear considerable blame too), but instead of stopping this disaster, we facilitated it.

More recently, our support of the Kuwaitis after the brutal dictator Saddam Hussein invaded them was commendable, and overwhelmingly appreciated by the local population. But if we'd acted more comprehensively, focusing more on the greater region rather than worry about the opinion of the world community/United Nations, our second war with Iraq would have been unnecessary. We should have removed the brutal Iraqi regime in 1991 once and for all.

I greatly admire President George H. W. Bush and supported his re-election. But at least in hindsight, not removing the Baathist regime (when we had half a million U.S. troops in the immediate area, including yours truly) was a mistake.

This variety of examples of international intervention and regime change have shown that peoples everywhere can be liberated, and the world made safer—if we act purposely, consistently, and in a timely manner. But we also should learn hard lessons about the dangers of being naive, unsure, or timid. We must have a clear philosophy and attendant policies if we are to protect others and ourselves from the dangers of a fallen world.

Applying these lessons to build a better world

I believe that God has entrusted America with our wealth, might, and bounty for a reason: to assist people everywhere to enjoy the same kinds of democratic freedoms we have—a liberty that yields individual responsibility and peace. Democracy won't be won without sacrifice, but freedom is worth the investment of blood and treasure. God wants us to enjoy our blessings—but serve as well.

Every time we leave our shores on a mission of liberation (at least in the long run) we become safer at home. Every time we eliminate a short-term threat to anyone on the planet, we eliminate a long-term threat to ourselves. This is win/win international policy. It will be hard work, cost lives and treasure and take a generation or more to accomplish, but in the end the world will be a community of free nations— reasonable democracies at peace with the United States and each other.

It is true that when you kick over a rock chasing a scorpion, you may find a viper ready to strike. But in a dangerous world we should anticipate this and be ready to meet new and expanded threats.

Remember, the snake was there anyway and had to be dealt with eventually. Better to deal with him on our terms than his!

It will take time to finish the immense job before us, but avoiding our responsibility with false hopes will only make the threats worse. There is no such thing as risk-free intervention. But if we are willing to pay a reasonable price (and yes, loosing 1000 soldiers to free 50 million people is reasonable), we can achieve a great deal of good and people might even thank us — but don't be in a big hurry for that one.

With this clear and certain philosophy as our mandate, the United States must continue to develop whatever military capabilities are necessary to remove tyrannical and oppressive bullies from our increasingly small planet. Doing so will encourage flowering of every positive aspect of liberty in both established and newly independent societies.

We should utilize our expanded military to descend on recalcitrant regimes like a cloud — an awesome force necessary to preclude the type of "second chance" opportunity being exploited by the scattered forces of Saddam Hussein and others seeking to take advantage of the follow-on phase of the current war in Iraq. We certainly had adequate forces for the "shock and awe" phase of the operation, but I hope we have learned an important lesson: without a larger force to envelope the defeated army, they can melt away to fight again. We must have additional follow-on forces sufficient to police the entire nation and disarm the bad guys — at least until indigenousness entities, both military and police, can be organized, trained, and deployed to protect the new society.

We should help rebuild every newly formed democracy in the image of all truly free and independent nations, and we should stay by their side for a generation or more until the young democracy can stand on its own. We must help each liberated people draw on the best of their past, and meld these historical strengths with the best of the new ideas we enjoy here in the 'land of the free'.

We should invite the best and brightest of the world here for training, and then ensure that they return home as ambassadors of mutual good will. We should build up the educational infrastructure of our new friend so that it graduates teachers, doctors, scientists, and others who will serve with distinction. This enlightened longterm strategy will facilitate development of a new generation of leaders friendly to America, and contribute to the development of an adequate cadre of competent leaders that will lead future generations toward peace and prosperity.

Positive Unilateralism

I advocate investing our own resources to help these potential democracies, budgeting whatever funds are necessary to pay for both the liberation and follow-on infrastructure development phases. However, following successful completion of the war, and after they have rebuilt their infrastructure (utilizing American and coalition contractors in proportion to each allies' sacrifices) to the point where their primary needs are met, we should expect them to repay our investment in full. This is practical and will build up the self-esteem of our new friend and ally. This effort will be directed by the first generation of leaders we select to lead the transition to their version of full democracy.

Over the course of a generation (and I strongly advocate looking long-term), America will not only receive back all of the funds invested in the initial military campaign that liberated the oppressed nation and created the new democracy, but we will receive funds (or lower-priced commodities) to cover all infrastructure investments and the long-term military and civilian presence necessary to guarantee long-term stability. The end result will be another lighthouse of democracy in an increasingly brighter world, and a mutually profitable, long-term trading partner.

This approach combines the best of idealism and practicality, altruism and self-interest, and it should have broad appeal—not only among a majority of Americas—but also in the newly liberated nation, and among our international friends. Partner nations that joined our coalition will share in the post-war blessings on a proportional basis. This is the essence of positive unilateralism.

Doing what we can

I want to emphasize that my philosophy and attendant policies advocate proactively seeking out and eliminating evil wherever it manifests itself—but only to the extent that we have the resources to do so. We will remove people and organizations that are committed to attacking America and our allies, and the world will be safer as a result. However, our current, relatively small military only encourages oppressive adventurism and destabilizes our vulnerable planet.

On the other hand, though I obviously advocate taking measured risks, I am against the kind of unnecessarily risky, even self-destructive idealism that President Kennedy expressed in his inaugural address when he said "let every nation know, whether it wishes us well or ill, that we shall pay any price, bear any burden, meet any hardship, support any friend, oppose any foe, in order to assure the survival and the success of liberty".[1]

We should never engage in any action without carefully weighing the costs (in business terms: doing a cost/benefit analysis) to determine both short and long term outcomes. There are some projects, though idealistically worthy, that are simply too costly. For example, what can we do to facilitate Russia's abandoning its nuclear weapons program? I advocate working with them as a cautious friend, a new friend who has taken important steps along the road toward full democracy.

But we would create chaos if we tried to force them to disarm—a move that, at the least, would lead to a renewal of the Cold War, and at worst lead to nuclear war. But we certainly can and should work with Russia to help it transition to a more modern, safe, and smaller nuclear arsenal—and along the way purchase as much of their stockpiles of fissionable material and related technology as they are willing to sell, and hire as many of their brilliant engineers as are willing to be hired—a policy that keeps both the material and the scientists out of the hands of terrorists and rogue states. We are doing both now with considerable success, and remember, since it only takes a few pounds of certain materials to make a lethal dirty bomb, time is of the essence.

In this dangerous world, particularly in third and forth world societies, we can intervene for mutual benefit as we have successfully done in Iraq and Afghanistan. We should create a systematic policy that evaluates every country to determine their level of democracy or oppression. Then we should approach them diplomatically and offer to help them transition as needed. If these efforts fail, we must intervene militarily where practical.

We must have a lager military. I am against risking our safety by maintaining a small military in the vain hope that unilateral love will break out and spread across the planet. The smaller our military, the more aggressive the evil of this world will be to dominate and exploit others. We are not, and should never be, a bully. But we should bully the bullies, and rid the earth of them.

Currently, the United States military has about one and one half million personnel in all services on active duty. I advocate increasing our force to two million professionals, and augmenting these with four million mandatory national service personnel (MNS). 95% of the MNS personnel will serve two years, and the rest will become officers and serve four years. This combined force of six million is far less than the sixteen million military personnel that served during WWII, but our technology will compensate for the difference. National service is presented in the 5th Pillar of Freedom.

Increasing our force structure will eliminate the current problem of relying too heavily on reserve and national guards units— forces I believe should be called up only in domestic crises or in true large-scale wars where these citizen soldiers will tip the scale toward victory. Also, since active duty personnel are over-deployed now, increasing the military to six million personnel will spread the load in a much fairer way. Removing excessive burdens from active duty personnel will greatly enhance retention of both officers and enlisted ranks.

We can't seek out and eliminate terrorists and rogue nations without sufficient personnel and technology to do the optimum job. Having an optimum force structure and necessary accompanying infrastructure (air and sea transportation capability, airfields and ports, plus the civilian manufacturing facilities to support them) will enable us to preempt most enemy action before it happens. With appropriate force levels our diplomatic corps will be tremendously empowered. Victory without combat comes from a powerful peace-time military. We cannot underestimate the intimidation factor of an expanded United States military: like Libya, self-preservation will lead to positive internal political change. However, if the use of force becomes necessary, a large force will enable us to crush enemy forces quickly saving both our lives and theirs.

As for abandoning our hard won sovereignty by handing over control of our deployed military forces to the United Nations, let me be clear: this is as damaging a move as we could conceive and I am totally against such a philosophy or policy. I am all for accepting the help of like minded allies in a joint operation—those who choose to join our unilateral efforts to eradicate evil. But there is a vast difference between cooperation and capitulation.

Additionally, we must not tolerate civil disruptions during the psychologically significant post-combat occupation, nor any kind of illegal activity during the infrastructure development or training phases that follow. Transitioning from a totalitarian state to a democratic one will take time, and these efforts require an atmosphere of peace.

American forces must utilize local police and military capabilities as necessary, and also help develop a new and expanded societal infrastructure, including a new school system that teaches kids to appreciate their own hard won freedoms and the friendship extended by the United States. We will also help the new democracy develop its police and fire infrastructures, and rebuild their military as an effective American ally in the region.

Specific countries that need to change their aggressive policy of seeking destabilizing weapons of mass destruction are North Korea, Iran, and Syria. These three regimes are threats to the United States, and our close friends Israel, South Korea, and Japan.

Of vital importance, we must not move irresponsibly or in haste. As we survey and interact with our needy world, we must gather accurate information, and if action is warranted, invite a broad range of allies to join us. This policy and action plan will create positive momentum, and will result in freeing hundreds of millions of people from tyranny, plus remove serious threats to American citizens. The goal should be nothing less than obtaining the most comprehensive peace possible in our hostile world!

Intelligence Capabilities

Fellow Americans, our tremendous resources give us a leadership position in the world unheard of in history, and we should exercise our responsibilities accordingly. Though there have been dominant world powers before us, none viewed themselves primarily as world peacemakers (even our friend Great Britain was a dominate colonial power) and no world power had our technology. Therefore, to enhance our ability to lead effectively, I also advocate increasing our superb intelligence capabilities—especially expanding the human intelligence component of our information-gathering infrastructure. The budgets of the various agencies must be increased accordingly, and in general, I support the recommendations of the 9/11 Commission that looked into the intelligence failures leading up to the terrorist's attack.

One of the key intelligence failures lies with those American leaders who have been under-funding our intelligence community, and under-utilizing or even bad-mouthing this group of professionals for years. At the feet of such critics lies much of the responsibility for our current situation.

Israel and Taiwan

I advocate maintaining the closest possible relations with these two friends and allies. America's position has been, and should continue to be, that any military aggression that threatens the existence of either of these nations will be considered the same as attacks on the United States itself!

Israel

Israel has been a Jewish state since 1446 B.C. when Joshua led the Hebrew nation across the Jordan River and conquered the land God had promised to Abraham five hundred years before. Israel was a recognized sovereign nation in the region for fifteen hundred years after that, enjoying various degrees of independence until its destruction by the Romans (A.D. 70 through 73).

Since that time, there has always been a Jewish presence in Israel, even as one wave of conquest after another drew and redrew the boundary lines of Middle Eastern empires—up to and including the Twentieth Century. These powers included the conquering Moslems, Ottomans, and the British, but none of these displaced the permanent Jewish presence. Additionally, the Jewish peoples scattered throughout the world during the Diaspora never forgot their biblical/historic/geographic roots, and always longed to return to their homeland.

The British Balfour Declaration during World War I recognized the re-establishment of a Jewish homeland in ancient Israel, a natural acknowledgement of the Zionist movement that began in the nineteenth century to encourage Jews to return home to what the Romans had insultingly named Palestine (they named the area after the Philistines, Israel's mortal enemy). After World War II, the British government finally withdrew is forces and flag from Israel, and in 1948 Israel became a nation again.

In 1948, as a re-created and independent member of the community of nations, Israel resisted militarily superior Moslem neighbors that attacked from all sides. Israel was victorious in that and three subsequent wars (1956, 1967, and 1973) and have consolidated their existence since then—relying heavily on American support to grow into the flourishing democracy it is today.

We should continue to provide whatever assistance Israel needs to maintain a democratically elected government in this dangerous region. We fully support the right of Israel's neighbors to exist as well, and we should use as much influence as we can to help them transition into multi-party democracies with freedom of religion and other basic human rights.

America should also encourage Israel to continue to recognize with full citizenship rights, anyone who is committed to live in Israel as peaceful and productive members of their diverse society, regardless of their religion or ethnicity. And we should support their democratically elected government.

The land within the current borders of Israel, including all areas of the so-called West Bank, Golan Heights, and Gaza are part of the historic nation of Israel and are under Israeli control today because invading forces from Syria, Jordan, and Egypt lost their battles of aggression.

Much of the region's national boundaries were artificially created by Britain during their colonial period, and should not supercede Israel's history or military victories. Throughout history, whenever a nation defended itself against an unprovoked attack by a hostile neighbor, and in the process of its defense captured that enemy's land, then the captured land rightfully belongs to the victor. The victor may elect to negotiate to give part or all of this territory back for some compensation or treaty rights, but they are certainly under no obligation to do so.

I support the establishment of Jerusalem in its entirety as the capital of Israel, and recommend that the United States maintain our embassy there.

Taiwan and the PRC

America should also continue to view the island nation of Taiwan as it is—an outpost of freedom only 100 miles from the communist Chinese mainland (the Peoples Republic of China). We should also support the Taiwanese people's decision to either become a stand-alone democratic state, or to reunite with the People's Republic of China—as they wish. But this latter option must be conducted within the context of the Taiwanese people's free will and not by PRC intimidation. Until we hear from Taiwan to the contrary, we should relate to them as if they were a fully independent nation, and we should help them militarily, economically, or otherwise as we would any close friend and ally.

That said, we should also strive for good relations with the PRC—within the framework of the other considerations mentioned elsewhere in this book. We should continue to trade with them, but on a more mutually beneficial basis, understanding that our trading relationship with the PRC and other one party nations helps build up a larger middle class that is the backbone of any (potential) democracy.

However, we should restructure our business relationship with China to better meet our own needs. One of the key factors affecting our future trading relationship with the PRC is our adoption of the new national sales tax discussed in detail in the 4th Pillar of Freedom. Our new tax structure will make our exported goods more competitive, create more jobs here at home, and reduce our trade deficit. The current system works in China's favor.

A brief aside: *Because the new U.S. national sales tax I recommend in the 4th Pillar will not be applied to exports, and because other hidden taxes will be removed from the base price of all goods and services, the new base price will be about 25% lower. The new price of exports will cause demand for them to surge everywhere in the world.*

Ask this question: what would a 25% drop in prices do to our exporting sector? The answer is that we would experience a dramatic surge in exports—creating additional jobs and wealth for American workers and business owners. And as the overall economy grows, the tax base broadens and both state and national sales tax rates will drop. This is exciting stuff!

We also need to be more fervent in pressing China to stop its massive abortion campaign, and to stop exporting arms to those countries who would hurt the United States or our allies. My proposals for an upgraded diplomatic effort—empowered by a significantly larger and more powerful military—combined with our dynamically improved trading equation, will help us achieve these two vital goals with the PRC.

Strategic protectionism and free trade

I support current business laws that provide orderliness in the international market place, a sector where millions of Americas derive their livelihoods. Anti-trust laws should be enforced equitably because we want a market place characterized by competition and innovation. I also support free and fair business practices that include free trade—as long as it doesn't undermine our national security, sovereignty, or strategic infrastructure.

But we should not participate in any international treaty that weakens our ability to provide for our own strategic needs, or that damages our sovereign responsibility to defend our vital interests worldwide.

For example, government contracts for steel should be let to domestic producers first, exhausting our own resources before turning to imported steel. However, the civilian market (that portion of which is not part of the infrastructure that produces our ships, tanks, planes, ports, airports, etc.) should take advantage of lower priced steel and other strategic materials or machinery manufactured by foreign entities.

But for our vital strategic needs—where our own production may be the only sources we have in wartime—we must protect our domestic producers to ensure that they can produce at optimum capacity. This is not a jobs program or classic protectionism, but rather it is a policy that should extend to any vital industry—a concept I call "strategic protectionism".

Experts in business and government should be convened to determine what the strategic production levels should be in every vital industry. Once certain industries are adequately protected, we should engage in free trade in every sector or commodity as we do today. It is probable that we will spend more to produce domestic steel to build our aircraft carriers and other strategic necessities, but we can't afford to be dependent on outside sources for any critical needs, be they military or healthcare related.

Additionally, we must be extremely careful to think through the implications of our high technology—determining their strategic importance before allowing their export, even to friends. It would be a tragedy if terrorists or rogue nations got their hands on our technological breakthroughs and used them against us (as nuclear weapons technology got away from us and are a continual threat today).

Further, we should reexamine existing treaties of all kinds—evaluating their strategic implications. We must not allow ourselves to be entangled in any international treaty or relationship that permits outsiders to veto any mutually beneficial trade agreements we negotiate with other sovereign powers, nor to negatively impact our international trade. We will negotiate with trading partners on an individual or collective basis as appropriate, specifically supporting NAFTA and other trade agreements only to the extent that they don't threaten our own producer's ability to meet our strategic needs. We must apply this philosophy to every economic sector, be it manufacturing, agriculture, or high technology.

We must modify or eliminate any current agreement that exposes us to dangerous strategic risk. We must ask the following question: what would happen to us if this or that commodity were suddenly cut off during a war? If we can live comfortably without it, then it shouldn't be in the strategic category. But if we couldn't defend or feed ourselves because country X decided to cut off a certain commodity, then we must anticipate that now and take appropriate steps to remedy the situation before it becomes a crisis. Think oil or steel in wartime!

Energy policy

I also support a multi-generational conversion from fossil fuels to alternative sources of energy, a transition that will eventually replace our internal combustion engines. But even as this transition takes place over the next one hundred years because oil reserves are finite, we must protect our current sources of oil and develop new ones. The large military I propose will help in this vital economic area—effectively enabling our diplomatic efforts to maintain our sources of international supply even as we develop domestic sources. Our policy should ensure that oil is sold to us at reasonable prices (which we must help determine), and to act quickly and decisively if any political or terrorist entity threatens this vital economic lifeline.

I support a tremendous (and long overdue) program to build both oil refineries and nuclear power plants in the United States. The former will help keep the price of our gasoline and other petroleum products low, and the latter will provide a vital component of eventual freedom from fossil fuels. Clean coal is another alternative fuel that we possess in abundance in America, and fuel cells, wind and solar power—whatever our creative scientists can develop—all figure into our long-term calculation. However, since both oil and coal supplies are finite, we must earnestly plan for this transition now.

Policy Summary

America has been blessed beyond the expectations of our Founders. The implications of this include acting in mutual interest to help the world be as safe and as prosperous as possible. An organized pro-active international policy, including diplomatic efforts empowered by an optimal military force, will help us achieve these goals.

Notes

(1) President John F. Kennedy: Inaugural Address. Please see http://www.bartleby.com/124/pres56. html, page 2.

"Give to Caesar what is Caesar's, and to God what is God's."
Matthew 22:21 (NIV)

"Give to everyone what you owe him: If you owe taxes,
pay taxes; if revenue, the revenue; if respect, then respect;
if honor, then honor.
Let no debt remain outstanding, except the continuing
debt to love one another, for he who loves his
fellowman has fulfilled the law."
Romans 13:7-8 (NIV)

CHAPTER FOUR

The 4th Pillar of Freedom: A New Federal Tax System and Budget

Introduction

A merica's short-term federal financial situation is manageable, but our long-term prospects for continued solvency are grim.

Over the next seventy-five years we are dangerously under-financed to the tune of $51 trillion dollars[1], a dramatic shortfall caused mostly by the ever-escalating gap between our projected revenues and our ever-increasing obligations. These obligations include interest on the growing national debt, plus the Social Security and Medicare promises we've made to future retirees.

The retired population impacting this future budget shortfall includes 77 million members of the "Baby Boom" generation, and those who follow—all of whom are included in the seventy-five year budget projection cited above. As a result of the incredible financial demands that this large number of retirees will place on our budget, we have to anticipate a massive cash crunch that could bankrupt the national treasury.

Our current and projected federal budgets include successive years of hundreds of billions in deficit spending, a trend estimated to continue to add to our escalating national debt for years to come[2].

The set of solutions I recommend will significantly change our taxation methodology and budget priorities, and will phase out the larger socialistic aspects of our budget to save us from eventual bankruptcy. These program reductions are fair and phased in over many years.

But a further note of warning—the longer we wait to fix this systemic problem, the more dangerous it becomes.

Compounding these problems, our current income tax system is fundamentally unfair. It negatively impacts savings, investment and productivity; wastes billions of hours of our citizen's time; and is wholly unequal to the task of meeting projected needs. This dysfunctional system's waste and inefficiency costs our economy hundreds of billions of dollars annually and contributes to our impending financial doom. Without significant changes to our federal tax system and attendant budget we have little hope of long-term solvency.

Fairness vs. socialism

"Throughout most American history, 'fairness' has meant 'equal treatment under the law.'"[3] "With the introduction of a socalled progressive income tax, this definition was abandoned [and the idea of fairness changed to mean] 'ability to pay.' Thus, the tax code stopped being simply a mechanism to fund the operation of the federal government. Instead, it became a tool for politicians to redistribute wealth and fuel class conflict."[4]

It is my recommendation that our tax system be changed so that it once again treats citizens fairly by the classic definition cited above, eliminating the socialistic features that well-meaning leftists have forced on us for decades. These recommended changes address four major problem-areas that are contributing to America's economic woes: The first is our dysfunctional and counter-productive income tax system; the second is our imbedded socialistic entitlement programs; the third is our under-funded budget; and the forth is the need to cut our runaway spending.

The 4th Pillar provides real solutions to these four aspects of our looming financial crises. These solutions include replacing the income tax with a new national retail sales tax (which I have named the Dynamic Tax). Additionally, we should identify and phase-out as much of our institutionalized socialism as is practical, taking several decades to transition (out of fairness to those who, for one reason or another have come to depend on them). Also, we should up-grade and re-prioritize our federal budget.

We can comprehensively provide a significant level of benefits for all of our current, and soon-to-be-retiring poor and middle class seniors, and phase out the majority of our imbedded socialistic programs by the middle of this century.

Within two generations, liberty, responsibility, and individual and/or family long-term retirement planning will replace our massive socialistic federal entitlement programs, creating a society more like the one intended by our founders.

My recommended changes are reasonable and balanced, and give current teens a fifty-year warning to prepare for their own retirements—because by then, the Social Security and Medicare systems will themselves have been retired. Together, these two entitlement programs comprise about half of our current budget (and most of the projected future budget shortfall). Phasing them out will return retirement planning responsibilities to individuals, and will also save our economy from collapse.

Please see my recommendations in the 7th Pillar for more details on Social Security and Medicare reform.

No quick fix

We got ourselves into this predicament over the course of many decades, but with determination and patience we can eliminate the most destructive elements of our current system, and replace them with positive alternatives.

Legislation for the new tax system can be enacted within a few months, but the entitlement programs themselves (because so many poor retirees are counting on them as their sole source of retirement income and medical protection) will continue to pay current beneficiaries as long as they live. Additionally, new beneficiaries will be added over the next several decades, but the amount of Social Security and Medicare benefits offered will steadily diminish for those turning 65 after 2020.

A Brief Summary of the Recommended Changes

I recommend that all income taxes, payroll taxes, and most other federal taxes, be replaced with a national retail sales tax. This change will significantly improve the economy, and allow all workers to take home 100% of their wages. It will also create more and better jobs for the unemployed. The recommended tax rate is sufficient to meet our budget projection, and deficit spending, and will eventually provide enough surplus revenue to pay off our national debt. Additionally, the new revenue generation system will collect taxes in a more equitable way from a broader base of taxpayers.

There are two components necessary to improve our economy: A new national sales tax, and a new budget.

The first component:
Replace the income tax with a national retail sales tax, "The Dynamic Tax"

This first component of the 4th Pillar of Freedom will eliminate all income taxes, both business and personal, as well as all estate and gift taxes, all excise taxes whose costs are imbedded in current prices (i.e. the 43 cent per gallon average from state and federal gasoline taxes), all taxes on capital gains and interest income, and all payroll taxes. The Dynamic Tax replaces these revenues with a much fairer single consumption tax added to every **new** retail purchase of goods plus services. This new tax system allows workers to take home 100% of their paychecks and (as consumers) they will only pay the new tax when they make retail purchases.

Constitutional amendment

The 16th Amendment to our Constitution (which was legally necessary to allow personal income taxation in the first place) should be repealed as soon as possible. But it is not necessary to wait for this amendment to replace the current income tax system with the new national retail sales tax. The repeal process will take some time — but should be done to protect the country from returning to the counter-productive income tax.

This change in systems will enable the American economy to reach its full potential—releasing our job-creating business dynamo from its current constraints—and give the people increased levels of personal financial liberty and prosperity they've only dreamed of.

From our newly acquired levels of abundance and efficiency we will be better equipped to fund domestic needs, and be able to trade more productively with the rest of the world. We will also be able to afford the larger military we need to protect ourselves and our friends, and engage the world as discussed in the previous chapter.

A better system

Why is a new tax collection system necessary?" The answer is that the current system is unfair; has huge compliance costs; is biased against work, savings and investment; is inefficient; hurts exports; and is riddled with paternalistic social engineering.

But that said all that stands in the way of replacing this dysfunctional behemoth with a new and better tax collection system is an informed public that demands change. The people should seek out political candidates who champion this remarkable new vision, and elect and send them to Washington and to our state capitals to enact 7 Pillars' legislation.

Problems created by the income tax

Let's consider two areas where the income tax system negatively impacts our economy and lives. First, the income tax is grossly inefficient, wasting enormous amounts of our time: the average estimate is approximately 6 billion hours annually (that's **billion** with a **B**), but some estimates go as high as 10.2 billion hours—time spent just complying with the mountain of IRS rules and regulations.[5] I was very pleased that President George W. Bush mentioned this 6 billion hour figure during his acceptance speech at the end of the Republican Party's 2004 nominating convention. Our president advocates tax reform, and the Dynamic Tax takes reform to a new level of efficiency.

The cost of current wasted productivity is estimated at $300 billion dollars annually (more than $1,000 per citizen, per year).

Second, the IRS code has ballooned to more than 12,000 pages in length, and there are more than 200,000 pages of court opinions adding to the code's complexity. Both individuals and businesses invest enormous resources researching and complying with these statutes, and even those professionals who prepare taxes for a living labor to help us cope with the demands of this burdensome tax system.[6]

The solution is to adopt a better system that scraps the income tax at both the federal and state levels, and replace it with a simple and fair consumption tax that collects revenue every time consumers purchase new goods or services.

"Although the magnitude of the economic growth generated by a single flat-rate tax system generates lively debate among economists, the large marginal tax rate reductions in any NST (national sales tax) plan...combined with neutral tax treatment of savings vs. consumption, will have powerful positive effects on the economy. Work by Harvard economist (and Nobel laureate) Dale Jorgenson shows a 13 percent initial increase in the gross domestic product and a 9 percent long-range increase. Similarly, Boston University economist Laurence Kotlikoff predicts a 7 to 14 percent growth in national output within 20 years, about half of which occurs within 2 years."[7]

Transparency

Another benefit of scrapping the current tax system and adopting the Dynamic Tax is that it will be fully visible at every sale—there will be no hidden taxes forcing up prices. Every sales slip will have a line indicating the federal sales tax, just as is common in states today that have state sales taxes. The Dynamic Tax will be the only federal tax included in the price of your purchase or payment. No longer will hidden taxes "cascade" down through the price structure, inflating the price of your goods or services. Federal taxes will not be levied at intermediate (wholesale) levels of production.

"Businesses only collect taxes for the government in the form of higher prices or lower wages. Business taxes and compliance costs are simply costs of doing business that are reflected in their bottom line." These hidden costs are then passed on to consumers.[8]

A broad-based tax

Another aspect of fairness is that no new goods or services will be exempt from the new tax. All retail purchases will be taxed (except education which is treated as an investment in human capital), and farm produce consumed by farmers (which is just too small a category to inefficiently expend funds calculating). Cars, houses, food, clothing, medical care, lawyer fees—every **civilianpurchased** good or service is part of the tax base—a broad base necessary to keep the rate as low as possible. But remember, only new goods are taxed. If any of the aforementioned goods are purchased used, they are tax-free.

A more stable tax base

Another benefit of adopting the Dynamic Tax is that consumption is a more predictable and stable tax base than income. "Consumption, over time, is more stable than income. When income falls or even ceases, people borrow, dip into savings, or rely on gifts to maintain consumption levels. Similarly, when income is unusually high, people tend to either pay down existing debts, or to save more.

"It is indeed preferable to have a federal tax base that is relatively stable. A stable tax base gives rise to smaller variations in government revenue over time. A steady flow of revenue allows the government to more effectively budget and more easily avoid running deficits."[9]

Required revenue and a necessary tax base

There are a number of ways a consumption tax can collect revenue, but I recommend the following:

The tax base

The tax base will consist of every new good or service purchased at the retail level. Government purchases are excluded (unlike some alternate plans), but at any point where the government competes with the private sector, sales tax will be added to the sales price of these new goods and services as well.

Exports produced by both government and civilian sectors are excluded from sales tax. This rule will greatly enhance our international commercial competitiveness, especially when compared to foreign producers whose governments may have subsidized their exports. As previously mentioned, I treat education as an investment and do not tax this sector. If, however, the majority of our citizens want to broaden and flatten the tax base further by including the education sector, so be it.

The resulting 2005 tax base is $4.5 trillion dollars (about half of our projected 2005 Gross National Product minus the 25% in hidden taxes which the new system eliminates).

The Amount of Revenue Needed

Once the tax base is determined, the next step is to determine the amount of revenue needed to meet our budget commitments. To determine this figure, look at the projected expenditures in the president's 2005 federal budget which totals $2.4 trillion dollars, or look in my budget to see that I recommend a slightly higher (5.5%) 2005 outlay (including interest on the national debt). These figures are the revenue goals. It is important to note that, in the long run, the changes I recommend will greatly reduce the budget in real terms — with accompanying reductions in the federal sales tax rate as well.

One problem with the president's 2005 budget is that it reveals a revenue projection that includes a $350 billion deficit (shortfall), following a more than $500 billion deficit in 2004 (these figures are estimates and will become definitive after additional time and analysis by government accountants in the Congressional Budget Office).

Clearly the current system is not bringing enough revenue into the national treasury to pay our bills. Obviously we could slash our spending to match current revenue, and in the long run it is vital to eliminate unnecessary spending—but I recommend that we do this on a gradual basis. The current budget includes the dual contexts of war and longterm socialistic program dependency, and I believe the more prudent and fair way to reduce our real spending is to do so gradually. This methodology gives people reasonable time to become self-sufficient—and helps non-profits and charities to have more time to build up resources to help people who are experiencing difficulties.

With the tax base and revenue goals determined, the next step is to determine the tax rate. The required tax rate is explained in the following discussion of price structure.

Prices

How prices will be impacted by the new tax system is vitally important and of great interest to every consumer. The bottom line is that prices will increase after the new tax system is implemented, but these increases must be evaluated in light of the tremendous good that will result from the change.

Since hidden taxes are included in all current prices, their removal under the new tax system will cause the base price to drop—and prices will only increase relative to the new base price. For example, when hidden taxes are removed from a loaf of bread currently priced at $1.00 (with hidden taxes estimated to average 25% of current prices), the new base price would be $0.75.[12]

The Dynamic Tax must determine a tax rate necessary to raise the $3 trillion in revenue needed to meet my recommended budget. Though $3 trillion is more gross revenue than apparently necessary, we have to anticipate non-compliance losses, and include state and retailer collection fees. To raise $3 trillion dollars from a tax base of

89

$4.5 trillion dollars, the initial tax rate must be 67%. Let's apply it to find the new price of our bread.

First we multiply the bread's new base price of $0.75, by .67 to get the amount of tax ($0.5025 is rounded down to $0.50). The next step is to add the tax (50 cents) to the new base (75 cents) to get the new price: $1.25. This new price raises the amount of proportional revenue necessary to achieve our larger revenue goals.

Consumers should remember that this 25% price increase is part of the new system that allows everyone to take home 100% of their paychecks!

Revenue neutral?

The phrase and concept of "revenue neutrality" is used in other consumption tax systems. By this, proponents seek to establish a tax base and rate that will yield the same amount of federal revenue as is received today. They are not trying to bring in enough revenue to meet the current budget.

However, I recommend that the Dynamic tax' initial rate not only bring in the revenue required to meet our current obligations without a deficit, but, in addition, it should bring in a small budget surplus to begin paying off our national debt [currently estimated at

$4.5 trillion dollars ($7.5 trillion on the national debt clock), requiring annual interest payments of $178 billion]. I further recommend accumulating surpluses until we both pay off our debts, and establish an adequate contingency fund for future national emergencies.

Finding the right balance

Fairness can mean different things to different people. It can be used by socialists to "help" people so much that the result is multigenerational dependency on the federal government. It could also mean slashing socialistic programs immediately—effectively jerking the rug out from under those who are now dependent on federal and state government programs.

The budget I propose will not be radical in either extreme. It includes reductions in some areas of the current budget (some which begin immediately, while most others are multi-year phaseouts). Some are increased. Each change is designed to meet particular needs and priorities as America grows and deals with our hostile world.

Four areas have significant adjustments: defense, education, Social Security and Medicare. The new federal budget better meets the demands of America's 21st Century role in the world. Discussions of the philosophical reasons underpinning each recommended change are included for each government department. Of significance, Social Security and Medicare, whose combined sub-budgets comprise about half of the current federal budget, are each generously funded for current and soon to be retired Americans, before being subsequently phased out starting in 2021.

People retiring after 2020 will be added to both programs until 2052 with diminishing benefits, but after that final year, no new retirees will be added to either program. Both programs will pay benefits to each qualifying retiree for the rest of their lives. This timetable and strategy gives today's teenagers approximately 50 years to budget and save for their retirements.

Larger Purchases

There will be a payment mechanism built into more expensive purchases like houses and cars, giving the purchaser the option of spreading the sales tax out over the life of the payment schedule (with low interest). Should the house or car be sold before the tax is fully paid off, the new owner will only inherit responsibility to pay the remaining portion—avoiding double-taxation. Except for taxes still owed at the time of the changeover from the income tax to the Dynamic Tax, all existing goods will be treated as if the tax had already been paid.

When new houses are purchased under the new system, only the principle is liable for the sales tax. Monthly mortgage payments may be stretched out over the life of the loan as per current practice. Mortgage interest is tax-free. Interest rates on the delayed sales tax will be very low — probably pegged at the rate the government must pay for its cheapest bonds.

All existing property improvements will be deemed to have paid the sales tax at the time the new system takes effect, minus any existing deferments of any taxes due at the date of the change.

Property taxes

I recommend that property taxes be repealed, and the revenue they generate replaced with specific use taxes such as fire or police protection taxes, etc. Cities or counties could adjust their own sales taxes to cover these services, or homeowners could be charged a per household fee for each service. Unimproved land sales should not be taxed.

Wages and Investment

The business and worker-friendly Dynamic Tax will positively impact investment, powering real wages upward. This is vital because the availability of investment capital enables businesses to modernize and/or expand their manufacturing capability — thus securing and expanding the job base. The current system curtails investment and savings — capital formation at all levels — because of hidden "cascading" taxes. Once these accompanying taxes are removed, the now unencumbered capital can be invested, consumed, or saved — helping the economy in many ways.

Professor Dale Jorgenson "estimates that, after implementation of the sales tax, yearly real investment would initially increase by 80 percent relative to the investment that would be made under present law...The higher productivity caused by more investment per worker is one of the few ways to make U.S. goods more competitive while maintaining high living standards."[10]

"Foreign capital investment will also positively impact domestic wage rates in our economy. After repeal of the income tax, the U.S. will be perhaps the most attractive place on earth to invest. The U.S. will attract investment capital from around the world that will finance new plants and create jobs here in America. U.S. workers will build these plants, much of the equipment installed in the plants will be American made, and American workers will be employed in these plants to produce goods for both domestic and foreign markets."[11]

State taxes

When state taxes are added, prices will increase further, but will vary according to state. As part of the comprehensive switch from income to consumption taxes, I also recommend converting state income taxes to sales taxes. My home state of California is a high tax state, which currently charges consumers a sales tax rate of 6.00%. However, in most places the tax rate is over 8.00% because multiple layers of county, city, and district sales taxes are "piggy-backed" onto the state rate. California also has individual and corporate income taxes, plus other taxes. For ease of calculations, I am using a combined sales tax rate of 8.25%.

The personal income tax brings into the state treasury 39.1% of California's revenue, the corporate income tax brings in 7.8%, and the estate tax, which will also be eliminated when the Dynamic Tax is adopted, brings in 0.1% of state revenues. Therefore, when these three state tax revenues are converted to sales taxes, their converted and combined rate is 15.94%, rounded up to 16%.

Adding this current 8.25% state sales tax rate to the additional 16% yields a total sales tax rate of 24.25%.

If you multiply the base cost of our bread ($0.75) times the new state sales tax (.2425), you get the increased cost of the bread due to the new (combined) California state sales tax ($0.18).

To calculate the new cost of bread under the Dynamic Tax, you would add the new base cost of the product to the new federal and state taxes:

Base cost of the bread:	$0.75
Plus the Federal tax:	$0.50
Plus the California tax:	$0.18
Total:	$1.43

So now instead of the California consumer buying a loaf of bread for $1.00 plus an 8.25 cents state sales tax, the consumer will buy the same loaf for $0.75, plus a $0.50 federal sales tax, and a $0.18 state tax for a total price of $1.43 (a net increase of 35 cents). Not a bad deal when you consider the incredible benefits of changing tax systems so that everyone takes home 100% of their paychecks, investment profits, Social Security checks, Medicare checks, capital gains earnings, etc.

To these positives is added the great advantage of having a booming economy that produces more and better jobs and more stability. The bottom line is that all consumers will have a chance of earning higher wages, higher take home pay, more profits for their large and small businesses—while prices only rise about a third. A generation from now, when our federal debts are retired, the federal sales tax rate will begin declining and will eventually drop to 25%. Prices will drop accordingly.

Administrative concerns

As mentioned before, an important provision of the Dynamic Tax requires all states to conform their sales tax system to the new federal system. Only five states currently have no state sales tax, so nationally, there is tremendous familiarity with the sales tax system. In fact, 98% of the population lives in states where there is a state (or local: Alaska) sales tax.[13] Each state with an income tax will be required to convert it to a sales tax, and collect their non-fee revenue (like bridge tolls, etc.) via the sales tax.

Collection fees

Of great benefit to the states is the provision that 1% of the federal sales tax collected will be paid to each state as their collection fee. This makes the new law a funded mandate—a "dynamic" improvement over some of Washington's un-funded mandates! This provision makes it in the state's own best financial interest to carefully collect the new federal sales tax. Since most states already have sales tax collection mechanisms and infrastructures in place, adding federal sales tax processing will be little added burden.

Once collected, the states will forward this tax revenue to the U.S. Department of the Treasury on a monthly basis.

Initial tax collection

The tax will initially be collected at each retail point of sale. The store or business where the good or service was sold or rendered will collect the sales tax from transactions, and then forward the tax to the state on a monthly basis. Each retailer will keep 1% of the tax they collect, making it an attractive requirement—and every retailer a partner in the process.

It is important to note that there will be far fewer collection points under the new system. In California alone, 90% of the sales tax revenue is collected from just 10% of the retailers. This is additional evidence that the costs of complying with the new system will be dramatically lower.[14]

How will the poor fare under the Dynamic Tax?

Our American concept of fairness includes our treatment of the poor, and we have more than proven throughout our history that we do care, and we have consistently given time and treasure to help those less fortunate than ourselves. We have more than proved that we are a merciful and generous people, helping not only our own poor with their myriad attendant health, education, and housing problems, but also the poor of other nations. But the last thing we need are socialist legislators forcibly taking our money distributing it to whomever they choose.

However, it is good to know that the poor will also benefit from the new tax system. The Dynamic Tax will benefit the poor in two dramatic ways: First, the overall economy will be much better, creating more and better jobs. This means that those without jobs will be better able to find employment, and those who are currently working will have more job stability or more options to move up to better jobs.

Additionally, everyone will take home 100% of their paychecks, a positive development logically assisting the poor more than others.

Furthermore, under the current system, the poor pay hidden taxes and compliance costs, which will now be eliminated. The prices they will pay for their purchases will be elevated by about a third, but not enough to cancel the great benefits of having better jobs and more take-home pay.

Also, there is the added benefit (for poor and rich alike) of determining when the tax will be paid. Instead of the government invading everyone's financial privacy to determine the time of payment, under the new system each consumer makes their own tax-paying decision when they purchase new retail goods or services.

For decades many of our leaders have been enacting policies that are socialistic in nature (in this book defined as those cases where there is forced redistribution of resources from one person to another, i.e. government-directed charity). These officials, implementing their socialistic philosophies, have instituted ever-more-numerous tax laws to manipulate social policy. I advocate phasing out the overtly re-distributional elements of our federal budget (except for a medical "safety net" described in the Health and Human Services portion of the budget section). This phase-out will steadily return responsibility for people's lives to the people themselves. But beware, individual states may still choose to step in and continue all or part of the programs phased-out by the federal government. After all, we still live in a federalist system.

Charity

I support **voluntary** charity. My wife and I believe that we have an obligation to help our church and do other acts of family charity because of our religious faith and conscious. But this philosophy is very different from the kind of coerced "charity", which is one of the hallmarks of a socialist society. It is wrong for our neighbors—whom we elect to govern us under our democratic system—to morph themselves into Robin Hoods once reaching Washington, D.C. (or our state capitals), and begin forcing us, their fellow citizens who elected them, to do good works whether we want to or not. The inefficient history of welfare is an example of forced charity gone awry, and currently the federal government is budgeting an amazing $40 billion dollars just to feed American children. **The federal government should not be our parent.**

Socialism defies the philosophy of personal liberty. When government leaders force successful people to give their resources to those who are (not yet) successful, they are redistributing wealth. American law should be a framework within which people can work hard and strive to make themselves better, and choose to give to those less fortunate (as they desire) out of their abundance. Our laws should not revolve around the poor or those who fail—to the detriment of the productive. This is counter-productive to the goal of maximizing everyone's individual initiative and perseverance.

Regarding welfare, "A recent study shows that workers must earn $8-10 per hour to make as much as they would on welfare. How much more can we do and maintain any incentive to work?"[15] Every American with a conscious will help those who are disadvantaged, and the Dynamic Tax will help everyone have more disposable income with which to be generous.

But it is important to note that the poor breath the same free air as we all do, won at great cost by generations of fellow citizens on fields of battle here and around the world. Everyone should be obligated to contribute to our national defense and other critical needs on a proportional basis, because everyone benefits. The Dynamic Tax is a fair way for everyone to contribute proportionally to the national budget, a system where those whom consume little will pay little in terms of total dollars contributed, while those who consume much, will pay much. **But all pay at the same rate, a great incentive to be productive.** And everyone can take pride (as with universal national service) that they are making a contribution to the **general** welfare.

One objection raised in defense of the income tax is that it provides the major incentive to give to charitable causes (because of the tax-deduction provisions built into the current system). However, it is common knowledge that only a minority of the giving public itemizes their generosity on their tax forms. Perhaps most Americans give because they believe it is the right thing to do?

It is also pointed out that the Bible gives directives regarding charity, taxes and taxation. Please note however, that individual charity is always voluntary, while giving to the government is a requirement.[16]

Non-profits

Another question concerns treatment of non-profits under the new system. For these organizations, all dues and contributions will be given from pre-tax dollars instead of after-tax dollars, and the Dynamic Tax eliminates gift taxes. But any retail purchases, or sales conducted at retail, will be subject to the same taxes as any retail business. This rule prevents non-profits from having an unfair business advantage over for-profit enterprises.

How will seniors benefit from the Dynamic Tax and budget?

Of great benefit to seniors, the Dynamic Tax eliminates all capital gains and estate taxes. Additionally, senior's pensions and taxdeferred accounts face taxes under the current system, and only those taxes previously deferred and still owed will be subject to tax under the new system.

Income revenue from any source is protected under the new tax system. Seniors will only pay taxes when they make purchases of new retail items. Further, Social Security and Medicare payments are not taxed under the new system, and every senior is viewed as an individual when computing the amount of their entitlement payments. For a thorough discussion of recommended changes to the Social Security and Medicare programs, including my suggested monthly payments to each senior, please see the 7th Pillar of Freedom.

Seniors will pay for consumables like everyone else, but prices will have only increased moderately (per the earlier example of bread) because hidden taxes and compliance costs are eliminated.

Insurance

There are three major kinds of insurance: life, casualty, and health. The following is a discussion of how each of these will be treated under the new Dynamic Tax system:

Life insurance. All life insurance premiums contain an investment portion, which will be tax free, and a service portion (which is a consumption) requiring payment of the sales tax. Since the service portion of the premium is so small, and there are no direct payments to third parties (as may be true of a repair shop after a casualty claim), life insurance rates should be relatively stable. Once claims are paid, that portion of the payout that is consumed will be taxed. Those portions saved or invested will not be taxed until consumed at a later date.

Casualty insurance. As with life insurance, the service portion of the monthly premium will be taxed. But unlike life insurance, some claims are paid directly to the repair shop, while other policies pay cash directly to the beneficiary. Rates will be adjusted accordingly, but the repair shop will collect sales tax once (either from the insurance company or the customer), and the repair bill will reflect the new tax. Any non-service portions of the casualty premium will not be taxed, but the rate will be proportionally higher to reflect the higher costs of the relevant repairs.

Health insurance. The 6th Pillar of Freedom addresses health care reforms, but to specifically address the insurance portion of this larger issue, as with casualty insurance, only the service portion of health care premiums will be subject to tax. The premium's rates will reflect the new prices associated with the new system.

If the insurance company pays the medical bills directly, the insurance company will pay the sales tax (and presumably pass it along to the policy holder in the form of higher premiums). But, as with casualty insurance, if cash is paid directly to the beneficiary, then the beneficiary will pay the tax when they pay the medical bill.

My disagreement with the Fair Tax (and other NRST systems)

We could have a discussion of every area of American economic life and commerce, and present the Dynamic Tax implications for each one. But since this is not practical, and has been done well by the authors of the Fair Tax web site, I will only present a couple more examples to make my policies clearer. But I want to emphasize that I do disagree with these good folks in a few important ways.

The Fair Tax scholars make a good case for the benefits gained by switching to the consumption tax, and address the positive implications for most major sectors of our economy. I agree with much of their philosophy and policy, but disagree with them on three important areas: (1) eliminating poorer consumers from the tax base; (2) including the government sector in the tax base; and (3) on the low sales tax rate they estimate for the budget (because they use "revenue neutral" calculations).

These are three vital disagreements and it is my hope that professional economists and others will evaluate the relative strengths of each NRST system. I hope my book contributes to the sense of urgency that we need a national referendum on theses issues, and I believe the Dynamic Tax system will be proven more viable than alternate systems.

Rent

Residential rent is taxed because it is a form of retail consumption. Commercial rent is not taxed because it is a business expense, and will no longer cascade through the wholesale system adding to retail prices.

Collectables

Used collectables will not be taxed. New collectables will be taxed.

Summary

Americans are suffering under the current income tax system, but the Dynamic Tax will enable the economy to thrive. Every American citizen will be better off under this new system, as will everyone else in the world who benefits from a healthier American economy.

The second component: A new federal budget

We now move to the second component of the 4th Pillar of Freedom: current and future federal budget projections.

The president's 2005 budget lists $2.4 trillion dollars in planed expenditures, but only about $2.05 trillion in expected receipts. This projected deficit of about $350 billion dollars follows an approximate $500 billion dollar deficit in 2004. I propose a Dynamic Budget that collects enough revenue to meet our current and anticipated obligations, plus a modest amount of surplus revenue to begin paying down our national debt.

The new (Dynamic) federal budget:

This section will compare the president's 2005 budget with my Dynamic Budget. The current budgeting system contains "discretionary" and "mandatory" spending categories — the first category so-named because the president can modify and submit his spending proposals at his "discretion", while existing law determines spending requirements for the second category. I recommend that the mandatory category be eliminated, and that the entire budget be unified and adjusted at the discretion of the president (subject to the same post-submittal negotiation process with the congress that exists today).

The current budget is "unified" in the sense that it utilizes funds coming into Washington from various sources (including income taxes and other revenues, plus social security and Medicare payroll tax withholdings), but my recommendations will unify it even more. This enhanced flexibility will help the president adapt the budget to changing circumstances—particularly useful during the current long-term war against terrorism.

Under the Dynamic Budget some government department's programs are increased, some reduced, others phased out, and some eliminated. Federal departments will receive their revenues from the Dynamic Tax via the Department of the Treasury.

The departments of the federal government are presented in the order they appear in the budget, starting with the Department of Agriculture and ending with the Social Security Administration. Highlights of the Dynamic Budget include increases in the Departments of Defense and Education; program modifications (followed by eventual phase-outs) of the department of Housing and Urban Development, and the Social Security Administration; and phasing out the Medicare component of the Health and Human Services budget.

A projected seventy-five year federal budget (spreadsheet) is included at the end of this chapter, along with a chart and three (hopefully) helpful graphs. Except where noted, all monetary figures are expressed in millions of USD.

Federal Departments

Department of Agriculture

Total outlays in the president's 2005 budget: $81,778

This total is comprised of $20,781 in discretionary outlays and $60,997 in mandatory outlays. For the remainder of this budget section (unless otherwise noted), I am presenting the total (unified) budget figures, combining discretionary and mandatory spending.

Recommended changes

By far, the Food and Nutrition Service is the largest program funded under the Department of Agriculture. Since part of my goal here is to identify and either eliminate or phase out overtly socialistic programs from the federal budget, this program is targeted for gradual (10 year) elimination. People utilizing the various services funded by this program have been directly or indirectly encouraged to rely on them (instead of providing for themselves or seeking local assistance). For generations people have been encouraged to seek help from the federal government instead of relying on local resources if they are experiencing crises in their lives.

But it would be unfair to simply end these large government charities without giving the people dependent on them time to learn self-reliance during a reasonable phase out period. Ten years seems objectively fair to me, so my revised 2005 and future budgets reflect an annual 10% budget reduction until the Food and Nutrition program is fully retired in 2014.

To the extent that our society wants these types of programs to be funded and available to the poor who may need (short term) help, individuals or groups should create for-profit or not-for-profit organizations to meet these needs at local levels across the country— wherever charity minded citizens determine that needs exist.

Additionally, the Dynamic Budget recommends an additional 1% across-the-board reduction in 2005. However, there is an addition to the overall Agriculture budget to cover the department's portion of the $17,100 billion in annual spending that has been allocated on a percentage basis to each federal department from funds supporting the mandatory national service personnel that will serve their two years working for their assigned department. Please see the 5th Pillar for more details on mandatory national service (MNS), and see the MNS training costs chart at the end of this chapter.

The remainder of the Agriculture budget is unchanged, including the direct loan disbursements and guaranteed loan commitments that comprise the credit activity portions of the budget. These may be adjusted over the years as the agriculture sector changes in the future. Certainly the Dynamic Tax will positively affect this sector, because the entire economy will improve.

The new outlay for Agriculture is: $77,425

Department of Commerce

Total outlays in the president's 2005 budget: $6,151

Recommended changes

I recommend a 1% overall spending reduction. Proportional MNS spending is included in the new outlay.

The new outlay for Commerce is: $6,147

Department of Defense

Total outlays in the president's 2005 budget: $428,930

Recommended changes and additions

In order to fulfill our expanding obligations worldwide, the military must be much larger. This force expansion will be accomplished by increasing the number of career soldiers, sailors, air force, and marine personnel from current levels to two million. Additionally, half the MNS personnel (two million soldiers per two year service period—all volunteers) will be assigned to the military. The equipment procurement portion of the budget is also increased, so our troops will have more ships, tanks, aircraft, bases, etc., and the infrastructure to support them, as they sacrifice for our national defense.

The new DOD budget uses the president's 2005 budget as the base figure, and builds upon it. The mandatory national service, ROTC, and school vouchers programs are discussed more thoroughly in the 5th Pillar.

Additions to the 2005 DOD budget are as follows:

1. DOD portion of MNS training and service: $62,700
   a. Training costs calculated at $2,000/ month x
      3.8 million trainees x 6 months.

     b. Regular service costs calculated at $1,500/month
        x 3.8 million personnel x 6 months.

  2. MNS ROTC budget: $4,000
     a. Education costs calculated at $20,000/year x
        200,000 cadets.

  3. Additional equipment procurement: $50,000

The new 2005 outlay for DOD is: $545,630

Department of Education

In addition to the MNS school vouchers mentioned above which become effective in 2007, the new K-12 school voucher program totals (discussed more fully in the 5th Pillar) are reflected here.

Total outlays in the president's 2005 budget:	$64,342
Minus $52,706 from current unified budget outlays:	$11,636
Plus vouchers @ $3,000/K-12 student:	$156,000
Plus department's portion of assigned MNS personnel:	$1,265
Plus compensation to college level institutions for revenue lost due to the MNS program @$10,000 per student:	$38,000
The new 2005 outlay for Education:	$207,592

Department of Energy

Total outlays in the president's 2005 budget: $23,346

    The energy budget is not reduced. The new 2005 budget reflects only the MNS addition.

The new 2005 budget for Energy: $23,568

Department of Health and Human Services

    The Medicare portion of the department's budget presents the greatest long-range strain on the unified federal budget. Conversely, this program's phase-out produces the greatest long-term savings. The philosophical reasons for these changes are presented in the 7th Pillar and elsewhere. The budget changes are as follows:

Total outlays in the president's 2005 budget: $574,714

New Medicare total: $367,561

New USA Med program (replaces Medicaid/ SCHIP): $100,000

Discretionary outlays with 1% reduction: $65,890

"Other mandatory programs" total (5 year phase out): $27,111

MNS budget: $4,053

The new 2005 budget for Health and Human Services: $564,615

Department of Homeland Security

Total outlays in the president's 2005 budget: $31,024

    The Homeland Security budget is not changed, except to add its portion of the MNS budget.

The new 2005 budget for Homeland Security: $31,319

Department of Housing and Urban Development

Total outlays in the president's 2005 budget: $38,943

Programs to assist the poor in the areas of housing and urban development should be carried out at local and state levels by a mixture of private non-profit and for-profit groups, with gradually phased out state government assistance. Therefore, this budget calls for HUD to be phased out over ten years. It may be beneficial to maintain a relatively small national liaison office to facilitate communication between state programs, a service that can be budgeted and staffed toward the end of this ten-year phase out period.

Ten years is sufficient time to shift housing responsibilities to individuals via sales (or privately financed rental contracts where government housing projects are sold to investors). The context of these recommendations is a better economy where every worker will be able to afford necessities once the positive benefits of the Dynamic Tax take effect. Various private or state organizations and agencies will have ample time to increase their activities during this period.

State governments who wish to take upon themselves housing and urban development responsibilities being phased out by the federal government, will also have ample time to take over vacated administrative and infrastructure functions, and, if necessary, to raise state sales taxes accordingly.

This department is the only one to which I have not assigned MNS personnel and accompanying budget. If such personnel are needed during the phase-out period, this need can be negotiated with other agencies.

The new 2005 budget for HUD: $35,382

Department of the Interior

Total outlays in the president's 2005 budget: $8,883

The increased security needs of Interior, combined with its everincreasing acreage under management and assigned MNS personnel, account for its increased budget.

The new 2005 budget for Interior: $9,086

Department of Justice

Total outlays in the president's 2005 budget: $23,702

The security and crime prevention responsibilities of Justice require that its budget be maintained at existing levels. The slight increase comes from the department's share of the MNS budget.

The new 2005 budget for Justice: $23,927

Department of Labor

Total outlays in the president's 2005 budget: $57,006

The Labor budget is only reduced 1% because 90% of the mandatory portion of the current budget is unemployment insurance. Laborers throughout America will greatly benefit from the new Dynamic Tax because workers will take home 100% of their paychecks in a surging economy. Reductions in program needs will lead to reductions in the department's budget in the future, but will be calculated as they occur.

The new budget reflects the slightly reduced new base, plus the addition of the MNS allocation.

The new 2005 budget for Labor: $56,973

Department of State

Total outlays in the president's 2005 budget: $27,987

With the increased emphasis of engaging the world as recommended in the 3rd Pillar of Freedom, the U.S. needs more, not less, diplomatic resources—backed by a bigger and more powerful military. Combining a strengthened diplomatic corps, upgraded embassy operations world wide, and our military is part of my philosophy of peace through strength. Additionally, our state department will be even more important as our emotional and philosophical reliance on the United Nations diminishes.

The new 2005 budget for State: $28,253

Department of Transportation

Total outlays in the president's
2005 budget: $58,959

The transportation budget was reduced by 1%. When the MNS budget is added, the new total reflects a slight decrease.

The new 2005 budget for Transportation: $58,924

Department of the Treasury

Total outlays in the president's 2005 budget
(excluding interest on the national debt which will
be reduced as the dept is paid off): $52,232

The treasury department will be changed in several ways once the new Dynamic Tax system is adopted. Because of the shift from the income tax to the national retail sales tax, the Internal Revenue Service will no longer be needed. However, there will be some past collection and administrative issues to clear up, so I have budgeted a three-year phase out of this agency. The three-year phase out reduces the budget by $3.558 billion per year.

Additionally, three programs are immediately ended:

1. Payments where earned income credits exceed tax liability.
2. Payments where health care credits exceed tax liability.
3. Payments where child credits exceed tax liability. The budget is accordingly reduced by $ 41,382.

The new 2005 budget for Treasury: $17,457

Department of Veteran Affairs

Total outlays in the president's 2005 budget: $67,314

Veterans have paid a high price for serving our country. The least we can do is provide high quality care for those who were wounded and need special care, and for those whose service has caused great hardship during their later lives. The World War II and Korean War generations are retired now, and the Vietnam War generation will start retiring soon—increases reflected in the department's 2006 budget.

I envision that many of the MNS personnel assigned to help veterans will be trained as nurses. This will be another of the many win-win relationships created by the new MNS program.

The new 2005 budget for Veterans Affairs: $67,954

Corps of Engineers—Civil Works

Total outlays in the president's 2005 budget: $4,189

The federal government has tremendous responsibility for creating and maintaining many aspects of our river navigation, dams, and other national infrastructure systems. As these structures and systems age, the costs of maintaining them will place added burdens on the existing budget. In anticipation of these added costs,

I have increased the department's budget about 25%. Future civil engineers may come from MNS personnel who have done their stint in the department.

The new 2005 budget for Engineers and Civil Works: $5,048

Environmental Protection Agency

Total outlays in the president's 2005 budget: $8,277

As we come to grips with existing environmental damage, and seek to prevent further damage by enlightened privatization, the EPA will need an increased oversight budget to protect the public interest until private entities can assume these vital duties sometime in the future. Future environmental engineers may come from MNS personnel.

The new 2005 budget for the EPA: $9,086

National Aeronautics and Space Administration

Total outlays in the president's 2005 budget: $16,385

We must establish a research colony on the moon to harvest the scientific knowledge and tangible discoveries that will benefit mankind. (17) Additionally, a moon station will provide a better platform to launch deeper space initiatives, especially to Mars. Unknown wealth of various kinds awaits us, and we must press outwards. The budget has been increased accordingly. Future astronauts may come from MNS personnel.

The new 2005 budget for NASA: $20,190

National Science Foundation

Total outlays in the president's 2005 budget: $5,586

I am committed to most scientific inquiry—believing that the "trickle-down" benefits to our society are really a "cascade". However, I recommend that each line item in the budget be evaluated to ensure that the scientific inquiry is important and justified. The budget has been increased accordingly. Science interns will comprise the majority of MNS personnel.

The new 2005 budget for NSF: $6,057

Small Business Administration

Total outlays in the president's 2005 budget: $683

This is an agency that could be eliminated entirely. Though small businesses provide the majority of jobs in America, funding an SBA at the federal level is questionable. The last few presidential budgets have reflected a significant draw down, both in discretionary and mandatory components. I have left this agency budgeted to support research and maintain a federal liaison with the small business community—both for symbolic and substantive reasons.

Additionally, the agency will receive its portion of MNS personnel and attendant budget. Also maintained is the commitment to the guaranteed business loan programs. In the future, this entire endeavor may be defunded and transferred to state or local governments, (or better) to private entities.

The new 2005 budget for the SBA: $689

Social Security Administration

Total outlays in the president's 2005 budget: $544,052

An explanation of the changes in the Social Security budget is included in the 7th Pillar.

The new 2005 budget for Social Security: $559,451

Summary

The president's total budget for 2005 is $2,400,000,000,000 (in plain English: two trillion, four hundred billion dollars). However, because of the current income tax system, and the poor economy of the last few years, the projected receipts are about $2.05 trillion. This leaves a budget deficit of approximately $350 billion.

My recommended budget is 5.5% higher than that projected by the president, but importantly, the new Dynamic Tax system produces enough revenue to yield a small surplus instead of a large deficit.

The 2005 Dynamic federal budget: $2,532,774,770,000

Projected 2005 federal receipts: $2,590,000,130,000

Projected 2005 budget surplus: $57,225,360,000

Though these budget projections reveal that the Dynamic Budget increases spending by 5.5% in 2005, it projects an approximate 26% increase in revenue. This accounts for the projected budget surplus in 2005 of $57 billion dollars.

These projections accomplish several of the goals desired by changing from an income tax to a national retail sales tax, including increasing revenue sufficiently to pay our bills, replacing a deficit with a surplus (in most years) so we can begin paying off our national debt, making the tax base broader and fairer, and in the long-term, de-funding the larger socialistic aspects of the budget and transferring the responsibility of retirement and healthcare planning to the people themselves.

By 2035 the budget will be healthy enough to begin rapidly reducing the national sales tax rate. It will drop from the initial high of 67% in 2005 to a steady state of 27% beginning in 2073. Throughout the next seventy-five years, America will be the healthiest economy on earth.

Notes:

(1) Laurence J. Kotlikoff and Scott Burns, *The Coming Generational Storm: What You Need to Know about America's Economic Future*. The MIT Press, Cambridge, Massachusetts. Though the $51 trillion figure is on page 167, <u>this whole book is a must read</u> for anyone interested in tax policy and the future economic health (or lack thereof) of America.

(2) *Analytical Perspectives: Budget of the United States Government; fiscal year 2005*. U.S Government Printing Office. Washington, D.C., 2004 and *Budget of the United States Government: fiscal year 2005*. Washington, D.C., 2004. Both documents are available from the Government Printing Office or online. Please see <u>http://www.whitehouse.cov/omb/</u> <u>budget/fy2005/print/message.html</u> and other related sites for the president's budget message and associated documents.

(3) Please see a summary of the *National Retail Sales Tax Act of 1997*.

    a. <u>http://www.house.gov/tauzin/nrst-faq.htm</u>,   page   12. This article and others that compare and explain the relative advantages of a national sales tax may be found at Representative Tauzin's web site.

    b. For an historic (Eighteenth Century) look at thoughts on government taxation, please read *The Wealth of Nations*, by Adam Smith, The Modern Library, New York, 2000 edition. Book V, Chapter II, pages 879-980.

(4) Ibid. (Brackets mine). Also please see Professor Milton Friedman's classic work *Capitalism and Freedom,* The University of Chicago Press, Chicago and London, 1962. Especially see Chapter 1, "The Relation between Economic Freedom and Political Freedom", pages 7-21. <u>This book is a must read.</u>

(5) Please refer to the following Fair Tax website for more detailed information.

a. <u>www.fairtaxvolunteer.org/smart/future.html</u>, page 4. This wasted time will be drastically reduced under the Dynamic Tax system because no individuals will file returns. Additionally, only retailers will file sales tax reports (and accompanying sales tax-submissions)— about one tenth of those who currently file.

b. Also please see Sean Hannity, *Let Freedom Ring: Winning the War of Liberty over Liberalism.* Regan Books, New York, 2002. Mr. Hannity exposes the arbitrariness and counter-productivity of our current tax system in Chapter Ten, pages 206-227.

(6) I interviewed the well-known California accountant, Louis B. Frizzell, CPA, to find out if he would support a transition from our current income tax to a national retail sales tax. He was enthusiastic about eliminating the need to spend part of his professional time helping his clients deal with the complexities of the ever-changing income tax laws. He stated he would much rather spend all of his time helping his clients create new wealth. The interview was conducted on August 31, 2004.

(7) Please visit the Cato Institute website and read their extensive library...

a. The organizations of tax policy resources.The organization's online address is: <u>http://www. cato.org/cgibin/scripts/</u>

printtech.cgi/pubs/pas/pa-272.html, page 2. The parentheses are mine.

    b. Also please read: Dale W. Jorgenson and Kun-Young Yun, *Investment Volume 3. Lifting the Burden: Tax Reform, the Cost of Capital, and U.S. Economic Growth.* The MIT Press, Cambridge, Massachusetts and London, England, 2001. Please see especially chapter 8: "Fundamental Tax Reform", pages 317-408. This is an academic work complete with sophisticated mathematical proofs. However, there is also much to be gleaned by the layman looking for a comparison of the relative merits of the income tax and various consumption tax systems. The bottom line is that there is ample economic-model evidence to support shifting from the income tax to a consumption tax.

(8) Tauzin, page 5.

(9) Please see:
http://www.fairtaxvolunteer.org/smart/stable_gov_rev.html
pages 1 & 2.

(10) Please see: www.fairtaxvolunteer.org/smart/ investment.html. Page 2.

(11) Ibid.

(12) http://www.fairtaxvolunteer.org/smart/ sketch.html, page 1 "hidden income taxes currently make up 20% to 30% of all retail prices"

An additional point needs to be made here: It will take some time to settle in to the new tax base and rate. Some period of adjustment is obviously necessary. I recommend flexibility here both on establishing the best base and rate—each settling where it makes the best sense for our economy. Therefore I am not ready to fall on my sword to exclude the government sector from the base, but at least in my current thinking it does not make sense to require taxpayers to pay more for our federal goods and services, just to have a broader tax base. Whatever the eventual base, the sales tax rate and resultant prices will have to be sufficient to collect enough money to pay our bills.

(13) http://www.fairtaxvolunteer.org/smart/ stable_gov_rev.html, page 4.

(14) Tauzin, page 9.

(15) www.house.gov/tauzin/nrst-faq.htm, Page 1.

(16) Examples include voluntarily laying monetary gifts at the apostle's feet in Acts 5 1-11, so they could distribute them to the poor. In this instance, Ananias and Sapphira were punished for lying to God the Holy Spirit, not for withholding part of the proceeds from their land sale from the church. The context in this passage is clearly voluntary giving. On the other hand, God clearly directs believers to give as government entities require.

Please see Jesus teaching regarding paying taxes to Caesar in Mark 12:13-17, and his directions to Peter regarding the Temple tax in Matthew 17:24-27.

(17) Please see Harrison H. Schmitt, the *National Geographic* magazine, July, 2004. The article in the "World by Numbers" section by this famous geologist and Apollo 17 astronaut discusses many benefits of returning to the moon. Schmitt spent 22 hours on the moon in 1972, and is convinced the moon's soil contains helium 3, a rare isotope and key substance to enable fusion power.

MANDATORY NATIONAL SERVICE TRAINING COSTS
(All figures in billions)

2005	Department of Defense		Civilian Departments	
6 months of training	$	45.60	6 months of training	$ -
6 months of service	$	17.10	6 months of service	$ 17.10
	Total	*$ 62.70*	*Total*	*$ 17.10*
	Total: $79.80			

2006	Department of Defense		Civilian Departments	
6 months of training	$	47.91	6 months of training	$ -
6 months of service	$	17.97	6 months of service	$ 17.97
12 months of service	$	35.93	12 months of service	$ 35.93
	Total	*$ 101.80*	*Total*	*$ 53.90*
	Total: $155.70			

ROTC TRAINING AND 4 YEAR FOLLOW-ON SERVICE COMMITMENT COSTS
(All figures in billions)

Year/ Class	2005	2006	2007	2008	2009	2010	2011	2012	2013
1st	$ 4.00	$ 4.20	$ 4.42	$ 4.64	$ 5.80	$ 6.09	$ 6.40	$ 6.72	
2nd		$ 4.20	$ 4.42	$ 4.64	$ 4.87	$ 6.09	$ 6.40	$ 6.72	$ 7.06
3rd			$ 4.42	$ 4.64	$ 4.87	$ 5.12	$ 6.40	$ 6.72	$ 7.06
4th				$ 4.64	$ 4.87	$ 5.12	$ 5.38	$ 6.72	$ 7.06
5th					$ 4.87	$ 5.12	$ 5.38	$ 5.65	$ 7.06
6th						$ 5.12	$ 5.38	$ 5.65	$ 5.94
7th							$ 5.38	$ 5.65	$ 5.94
8th								$ 5.65	$ 5.94
9th									$ 5.94
Total	$ 4.00	$ 8.40	$ 13.25	$ 18.55	$ 25.29	$ 32.66	$ 40.71	$ 49.50	$ 52.00

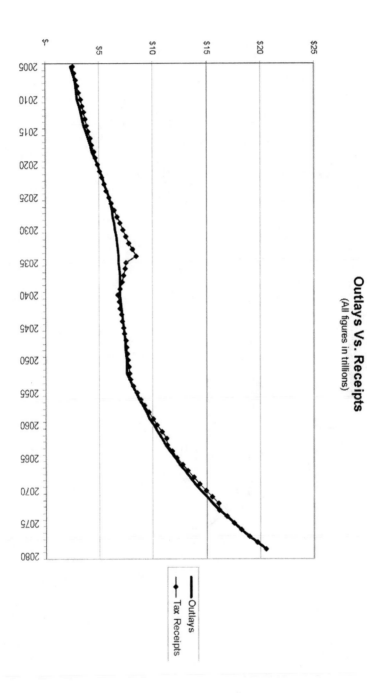

Outlays Vs. Receipts
(All figures in trillions)

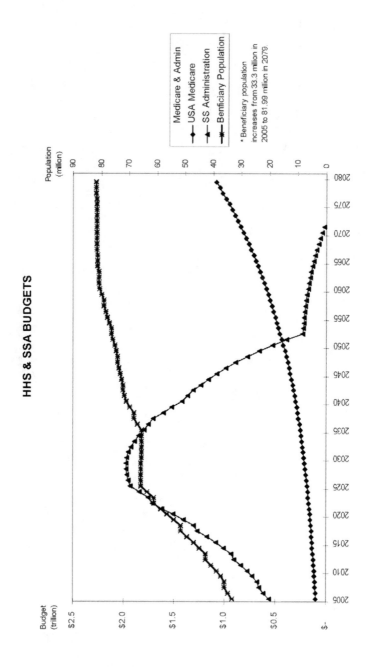

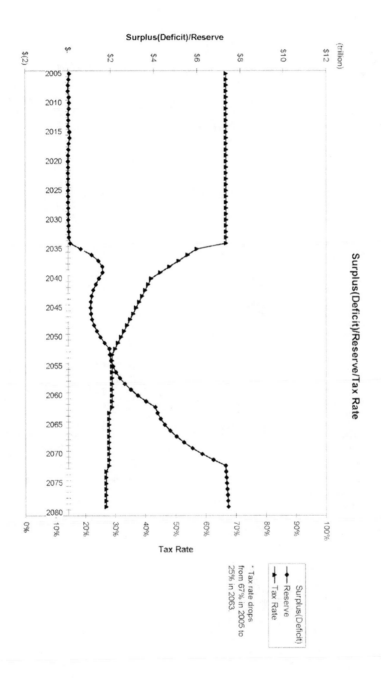

PROJECTED US GOVERNMENT BUDGETS
2005 - 2079
(All figures in millions)

Department	2005 Budget	2006 Budget	2007 Budget	2008 Budget	2009 Budget
Agriculture [1]	$ 77,425	$ 76,209.76	$ 73,255.90	$ 70,184.06	$ 66,856.32
Commerce	$ 6,147	$ 6,448.96	$ 6,636.05	$ 6,840.02	$ 7,050.49
Defense	$ 545,630	$ 607,625.84	$ 632,539.94	$ 658,630.69	$ 686,884.62
Education [2]	$ 207,592	$ 255,172.86	$ 357,218.12	$ 370,209.76	$ 339,715.98
Energy	$ 23,568	$ 24,726.13	$ 25,443.45	$ 26,225.50	$ 27,032.47
Health and Human Services [3]	$ 564,615	$ 600,906.83	$ 627,136.73	$ 638,799.31	$ 667,801.89
Homeland Security	$ 31,319	$ 32,858.02	$ 33,811.25	$ 34,850.51	$ 35,922.87
Housing & Urban Development [4]	$ 35,382	$ 33,408.87	$ 30,558.29	$ 27,560.37	$ 24,350.06
Interior	$ 9,086	$ 9,532.05	$ 9,808.58	$ 10,110.06	$ 10,421.15
Justice	$ 23,927	$ 25,103.17	$ 25,831.43	$ 26,625.41	$ 27,444.68
Labor	$ 56,973	$ 59,772.28	$ 61,506.31	$ 63,396.83	$ 65,347.57
State	$ 28,253	$ 29,641.48	$ 30,501.40	$ 31,438.93	$ 32,406.31
Transportation	$ 58,924	$ 61,819.55	$ 63,612.98	$ 65,568.25	$ 67,585.80
Treasury [5]	$ 17,457	$ 14,545.90	$ 11,090.23	$ 11,431.11	$ 11,782.85
Veterans	$ 67,954	$ 71,293.34	$ 73,361.61	$ 75,616.53	$ 77,943.26
Army Corps of Engineers	$ 5,048	$ 5,295.58	$ 5,449.21	$ 5,616.70	$ 5,789.53
Environmental Protection Agency	$ 9,086	$ 9,532.05	$ 9,808.58	$ 10,110.06	$ 10,421.15
NASA	$ 20,190	$ 21,182.32	$ 21,796.84	$ 22,466.81	$ 23,158.11
National Science Foundation	$ 6,057	$ 6,354.70	$ 6,539.05	$ 6,740.04	$ 6,947.43
Small Business Administration	$ 689	$ 723.38	$ 744.36	$ 767.24	$ 790.85
Social Security Administration [6]	$ 559,451	$ 616,114.99	$ 658,264.69	$ 678,497.77	$ 725,167.16
Total	$ 2,354,775	$ 2,568,268	$ 2,764,915	$ 2,841,686	$ 2,920,821
Interest on National Debt	$ 178,000.00	$ 178,000.00	$ 178,000.00	$ 178,000.00	$ 183,136.78
Total Outlays [7]	$ 2,532,774.77	$ 2,746,268.05	$ 2,942,915.00	$ 3,019,685.97	$ 3,103,957.32
Tax Base	$ 4,500,000.00	$ 4,725,000.00	$ 4,961,250.00	$ 5,209,312.50	$ 5,469,778.13
Tax Rate [8]	67%	67%	67%	67%	67%
Gross Sales Tax Receipts	$ 3,000,000.15	$ 3,150,000.16	$ 3,307,500.17	$ 3,472,875.17	$ 3,646,518.93
Non Compliance at 13%	$ (390,000.02)	$ (409,500.02)	$ (429,975.02)	$ (451,473.77)	$ (474,047.46)
State Collection Fees at 1%	$ (30,000.00)	$ (31,500.00)	$ (33,075.00)	$ (34,728.75)	$ (36,465.19)
Retailer Collection Fees at 1%	$ (30,000.00)	$ (31,500.00)	$ (33,075.00)	$ (34,728.75)	$ (36,465.19)
Customs Revenue	$ 20,000.00	$ 21,000.00	$ 22,050.00	$ 23,152.50	$ 24,310.13
Other Revenue	$ 20,000.00	$ 21,000.00	$ 22,050.00	$ 23,152.50	$ 24,310.13
Total Receipts	$ 2,590,000.13	$ 2,719,500.13	$ 2,855,475.14	$ 2,998,248.90	$ 3,148,161.34
Surplus (Deficit)	$ 57,225.36	$ (26,767.91)	$ (87,439.86)	$ (21,437.07)	$ 44,204.02
Debt Retirement [9]	$ -	$ -	$ -	$ -	$ -
Debt	$ 4,500,000.00	$ 4,500,000.00	$ 4,556,982.42	$ 4,578,419.48	$ 4,578,419.48
Cumulative Reserve	$ 57,225.36	$ 30,457.44	$ -	$ -	$ 44,204.02

NOTES:
(1) Agriculture: 10 year phase out of Food & Nutrition Program.
(2) Education: 3 year phase out of all mandatory outlays.
(3) Health & Human Services: Medicare phase out per schedule in the 7th Pillar of Freedom.
(4) Housing & Urban Development: 10 year phase out of department.
(5) Treasury: 3 year phase out of Internal Revenue Service.
(6) Social Security Administration: Department phase out per schedule in the 7th Pillar of Freedom.
(7) Outlay annual growth rate is 3%. Total receipt growth rate is 5% per year from 2005 to 2008 and 4% per year from 2009 to 2079.
(8) Debt fully retired in 2035. Tax rate drops in 2035
(9) End of year surplus used to retire debt. Interest reduction effective the following year.

PROJECTED US GOVERNMENT BUDGETS
2005 - 2079
(All figures in millions)

Department	2010 Budget	2011 Budget	2012 Budget	2013 Budget	2014 Budget
Agriculture	$ 63,252.25	$ 59,314.93	$ 55,087.59	$ 50,595.12	$ 45,739.17
Commerce	$ 7,266.85	$ 7,483.65	$ 7,707.10	$ 7,943.52	$ 8,180.76
Defense	$ 716,535.45	$ 747,658.93	$ 780,335.10	$ 807,584.83	$ 835,846.34
Education	$ 307,014.01	$ 318,509.60	$ 330,473.24	$ 343,190.53	$ 356,149.80
Energy	$ 27,862.02	$ 28,693.28	$ 29,549.99	$ 30,456.48	$ 31,366.08
Health and Human Services	$ 706,017.19	$ 754,525.21	$ 805,177.77	$ 829,877.69	$ 884,662.84
Homeland Security	$ 37,025.24	$ 38,129.89	$ 39,268.35	$ 40,472.96	$ 41,681.71
Housing & Urban Development	$ 20,914.42	$ 17,230.72	$ 13,308.89	$ 9,144.77	$ 4,708.94
Interior	$ 10,740.95	$ 11,061.40	$ 11,391.67	$ 11,741.13	$ 12,091.78
Justice	$ 28,286.89	$ 29,130.82	$ 30,000.60	$ 30,920.91	$ 31,844.37
Labor	$ 67,352.91	$ 69,362.38	$ 71,433.37	$ 73,624.68	$ 75,823.52
State	$ 33,400.77	$ 34,397.28	$ 35,424.30	$ 36,510.99	$ 37,601.40
Transportation	$ 69,659.83	$ 71,738.12	$ 73,880.05	$ 76,146.42	$ 78,420.56
Treasury	$ 12,144.43	$ 12,506.76	$ 12,880.18	$ 13,275.30	$ 13,671.77
Veterans	$ 80,335.14	$ 82,731.93	$ 85,202.10	$ 87,815.79	$ 90,438.45
Army Corps of Engineers	$ 5,967.19	$ 6,145.22	$ 6,328.71	$ 6,522.85	$ 6,717.66
Environmental Protection Agency	$ 10,740.95	$ 11,061.40	$ 11,391.67	$ 11,741.13	$ 12,091.78
NASA	$ 23,868.78	$ 24,580.90	$ 25,314.82	$ 26,091.39	$ 26,870.62
National Science Foundation	$ 7,160.63	$ 7,374.27	$ 7,594.45	$ 7,827.42	$ 8,061.19
Small Business Administration	$ 815.12	$ 839.44	$ 864.50	$ 891.02	$ 917.63
Social Security Administration	$ 774,003.98	$ 838,262.41	$ 905,477.28	$ 933,254.02	$ 1,006,126.81
Total	$ 3,010,365	$ 3,170,739	$ 3,338,092	$ 3,435,629	$ 3,609,013
Interest on National Debt	$ 183,136.78	$ 179,136.78	$ 175,136.78	$ 171,136.78	$ 167,136.78
Total Outlays	**$ 3,193,501.77**	**$ 3,349,875.32**	**$ 3,513,228.51**	**$ 3,606,765.71**	**$ 3,776,149.96**
Tax Base	**$ 5,743,267.03**	**$ 5,972,997.71**	**$ 6,211,917.62**	**$ 6,460,394.33**	**$ 6,718,810.10**
Tax Rate	67%	67%	67%	67%	67%
Gross Sales Tax Receipts	**$ 3,828,844.88**	**$ 3,981,998.67**	**$ 4,141,278.62**	**$ 4,306,929.77**	**$ 4,479,206.96**
Non Compliance at 13%	$ (497,749.83)	$ (517,659.83)	$ (538,366.22)	$ (559,900.87)	$ (582,296.90)
State Collection Fees at 1%	$ (38,288.45)	$ (39,819.99)	$ (41,412.79)	$ (43,069.30)	$ (44,792.07)
Retailer Collection Fees at 1%	$ (38,288.45)	$ (39,819.99)	$ (41,412.79)	$ (43,069.30)	$ (44,792.07)
Customs Revenue	$ 25,525.63	$ 26,546.66	$ 27,608.52	$ 28,712.86	$ 29,861.38
Other Revenue	$ 25,525.63	$ 26,546.66	$ 27,608.52	$ 28,712.86	$ 29,861.38
Total Receipts	**$ 3,305,569.41**	**$ 3,437,792.19**	**$ 3,575,303.87**	**$ 3,718,316.03**	**$ 3,867,048.67**
Surplus (Deficit)	**$ 112,067.64**	**$ 87,916.87**	**$ 62,075.36**	**$ 111,550.31**	**$ 90,898.71**
Debt Retirement	$ 100,000.00	$ 100,000.00	$ 100,000.00	$ 100,000.00	$ 100,000.00
Debt	*$ 4,478,419.48*	*$ 4,378,419.48*	*$ 4,278,419.48*	*$ 4,178,419.48*	*$ 4,078,419.48*
Cumulative Reserve	**$ 56,271.66**	**$ 44,188.53**	**$ 6,263.89**	**$ 17,814.21**	**$ 8,712.92**

123

PROJECTED US GOVERNMENT BUDGETS
2005 - 2079
(All figures in millions)

Department	2015 Budget	2016 Budget	2017 Budget	2018 Budget	2019 Budget
Agriculture	$ 47,103.12	$ 48,499.66	$ 49,939.15	$ 51,464.76	$ 52,993.49
Commerce	$ 8,424.71	$ 8,674.49	$ 8,931.96	$ 9,204.82	$ 9,478.25
Defense	$ 865,159.81	$ 895,567.14	$ 927,111.98	$ 959,839.87	$ 993,798.26
Education	$ 369,616.61	$ 383,564.60	$ 398,088.61	$ 413,550.19	$ 429,300.77
Energy	$ 32,301.42	$ 33,259.11	$ 34,246.25	$ 35,292.45	$ 36,340.80
Health and Human Services	$ 941,786.57	$ 1,007,475.19	$ 1,076,264.28	$ 1,109,143.33	$ 1,183,355.09
Homeland Security	$ 42,924.66	$ 44,197.32	$ 45,509.12	$ 46,899.38	$ 48,292.51
Housing & Urban Development	$ -	$ -	$ -	$ -	$ -
Interior	$ 12,452.36	$ 12,821.55	$ 13,202.10	$ 13,605.42	$ 14,009.56
Justice	$ 32,793.98	$ 33,766.27	$ 34,768.47	$ 35,830.62	$ 36,894.95
Labor	$ 78,084.59	$ 80,399.69	$ 82,785.99	$ 85,315.03	$ 87,849.28
State	$ 38,722.68	$ 39,870.76	$ 41,054.14	$ 42,308.31	$ 43,565.06
Transportation	$ 80,759.08	$ 83,153.48	$ 85,621.50	$ 88,237.18	$ 90,858.22
Treasury	$ 14,079.47	$ 14,496.90	$ 14,927.18	$ 15,383.19	$ 15,840.14
Veterans	$ 93,135.34	$ 95,896.67	$ 98,742.93	$ 101,759.45	$ 104,782.16
Army Corps of Engineers	$ 6,917.98	$ 7,123.09	$ 7,334.50	$ 7,558.56	$ 7,783.09
Environmental Protection Agency	$ 12,452.36	$ 12,821.55	$ 13,202.10	$ 13,605.42	$ 14,009.56
NASA	$ 27,671.91	$ 28,492.34	$ 29,338.01	$ 30,234.26	$ 31,132.35
National Science Foundation	$ 8,301.57	$ 8,547.70	$ 8,801.40	$ 9,070.28	$ 9,339.71
Small Business Administration	$ 945.00	$ 973.01	$ 1,001.89	$ 1,032.50	$ 1,063.17
Social Security Administration	$ 1,082,244.08	$ 1,170,980.03	$ 1,264,065.42	$ 1,302,681.65	$ 1,403,274.97
Total	**$ 3,795,877**	**$ 4,010,581**	**$ 4,234,937**	**$ 4,372,017**	**$ 4,613,961**
Interest on National Debt	$ 163,136.78	$ 163,136.78	$ 163,136.78	$ 163,136.78	$ 163,136.78
Total Outlays	*$ 3,959,014.06*	*$ 4,173,717.35*	*$ 4,398,073.77*	*$ 4,535,153.44*	*$ 4,777,098.17*
Tax Base	**$ 6,987,562.50**	**$ 7,267,065.00**	**$ 7,557,747.60**	**$ 7,860,057.51**	**$ 8,174,459.81**
Tax Rate	67%	67%	67%	67%	67%
Gross Sales Tax Receipts	**$ 4,658,375.23**	**$ 4,844,710.24**	**$ 5,038,498.65**	**$ 5,240,038.60**	**$ 5,449,640.14**
Non Compliance at 13%	$ (605,588.78)	$ (629,812.33)	$ (655,004.83)	$ (681,205.02)	$ (708,453.22)
State Collection Fees at 1%	$ (46,583.75)	$ (48,447.10)	$ (50,384.99)	$ (52,400.39)	$ (54,496.40)
Retailer Collection Fees at 1%	$ (46,583.75)	$ (48,447.10)	$ (50,384.99)	$ (52,400.39)	$ (54,496.40)
Customs Revenue	$ 31,055.83	$ 32,298.07	$ 33,589.99	$ 34,933.59	$ 36,330.93
Other Revenue	$ 31,055.83	$ 32,298.07	$ 33,589.99	$ 34,933.59	$ 36,330.93
Total Receipts	*$ 4,021,730.62*	*$ 4,182,599.84*	*$ 4,349,903.83*	*$ 4,523,899.99*	*$ 4,704,855.99*
Surplus (Deficit)	$ 62,716.55	$ 8,882.49	$ (48,169.93)	$ (11,253.45)	$ (72,242.18)
Debt Retirement	$ -	$ -	$ -	$ -	$ -
Debt	*$ 4,078,419.48*	*$ 4,078,419.48*	*$ 4,078,419.48*	*$ 4,078,419.48*	*$ 4,129,773.09*
Cumulative Reserve	*$ 71,429.47*	*$ 80,311.96*	*$ 32,142.03*	*$ 20,888.58*	*$ -*

PROJECTED US GOVERNMENT BUDGETS
2005 - 2079
(All figures in millions)

Department	2020 Budget	2021 Budget	2022 Budget	2023 Budget	2024 Budget
Agriculture	$ 54,569.27	$ 56,197.97	$ 57,881.94	$ 59,662.09	$ 61,460.79
Commerce	$ 9,760.08	$ 10,051.39	$ 10,352.58	$ 10,670.97	$ 10,992.68
Defense	$ 1,029,036.67	$ 1,065,606.71	$ 1,103,562.22	$ 1,142,959.34	$ 1,183,856.67
Education	$ 445,706.86	$ 462,834.02	$ 480,720.60	$ 499,729.23	$ 519,233.70
Energy	$ 37,421.40	$ 38,538.30	$ 39,693.10	$ 40,913.85	$ 42,147.33
Health and Human Services	$ 1,260,858.32	$ 1,335,433.62	$ 1,407,498.71	$ 1,436,427.92	$ 1,502,822.54
Homeland Security	$ 49,728.50	$ 51,212.72	$ 52,747.31	$ 54,369.54	$ 56,008.68
Housing & Urban Development	$ -	$ -	$ -	$ -	$ -
Interior	$ 14,426.14	$ 14,856.71	$ 15,301.89	$ 15,772.49	$ 16,248.01
Justice	$ 37,992.03	$ 39,125.96	$ 40,298.37	$ 41,537.74	$ 42,790.03
Labor	$ 90,461.50	$ 93,161.45	$ 95,953.03	$ 98,904.05	$ 101,885.83
State	$ 44,860.48	$ 46,199.40	$ 47,583.77	$ 49,047.20	$ 50,525.88
Transportation	$ 93,559.91	$ 96,352.34	$ 99,239.54	$ 102,291.63	$ 105,375.54
Treasury	$ 16,311.15	$ 16,797.98	$ 17,301.33	$ 17,833.43	$ 18,371.08
Veterans	$ 107,897.89	$ 111,118.26	$ 114,447.91	$ 117,967.74	$ 121,524.25
Army Corps of Engineers	$ 8,014.52	$ 8,253.73	$ 8,501.05	$ 8,762.50	$ 9,026.67
Environmental Protection Agency	$ 14,426.14	$ 14,856.71	$ 15,301.89	$ 15,772.49	$ 16,248.01
NASA	$ 32,058.08	$ 33,014.90	$ 34,004.19	$ 35,049.99	$ 36,106.68
National Science Foundation	$ 9,617.42	$ 9,904.47	$ 10,201.26	$ 10,515.00	$ 10,832.00
Small Business Administration	$ 1,094.78	$ 1,127.46	$ 1,161.24	$ 1,196.96	$ 1,233.04
Social Security Administration	$ 1,508,475.52	$ 1,613,311.64	$ 1,714,258.36	$ 1,750,112.74	$ 1,842,319.55
Total	**$ 4,866,277**	**$ 5,117,956**	**$ 5,366,010**	**$ 5,509,497**	**$ 5,749,009**
Interest on National Debt	$ 165,190.92	$ 170,727.62	$ 178,724.06	$ 188,820.51	$ 196,592.56
Total Outlays	***$ 5,031,467.58***	***$ 5,288,683.34***	***$ 5,544,734.34***	***$ 5,698,317.41***	***$ 5,945,601.53***
Tax Base	**$ 8,501,438.20**	**$ 8,841,495.73**	**$ 9,195,155.56**	**$ 9,562,961.78**	**$ 9,945,480.25**
Tax Rate	**67%**	**67%**	**67%**	**67%**	**67%**
Gross Sales Tax Receipts	**$ 5,667,625.75**	**$ 5,894,330.78**	**$ 6,130,104.01**	**$ 6,375,308.17**	**$ 6,630,320.50**
Non Compliance at 13%	$ (736,791.35)	$ (766,263.00)	$ (796,913.52)	$ (828,790.06)	$ (861,941.66)
State Collection Fees at 1%	$ (56,676.26)	$ (58,943.31)	$ (61,301.04)	$ (63,753.08)	$ (66,303.20)
Retailer Collection Fees at 1%	$ (56,676.26)	$ (58,943.31)	$ (61,301.04)	$ (63,753.08)	$ (66,303.20)
Customs Revenue	$ 37,784.17	$ 39,295.54	$ 40,867.36	$ 42,502.05	$ 44,202.13
Other Revenue	$ 37,784.17	$ 39,295.54	$ 40,867.36	$ 42,502.05	$ 44,202.13
Total Receipts	***$ 4,893,050.23***	***$ 5,088,772.24***	***$ 5,292,323.13***	***$ 5,504,016.05***	***$ 5,724,176.69***
Surplus (Deficit)	**$ (138,417.35)**	**$ (199,911.11)**	**$ (252,411.22)**	**$ (194,301.36)**	**$ (221,424.84)**
Debt Retirement	$ -	$ -	$ -	$ -	$ -
Debt	***$ 4,268,190.44***	***$ 4,468,101.54***	***$ 4,720,512.76***	***$ 4,914,814.12***	***$ 5,136,238.96***
Cumulative Reserve	***$ -***	***$ -***	***$ -***	***$ -***	***$ -***

PROJECTED US GOVERNMENT BUDGETS
2005 - 2079
(All figures in millions)

Department	2025 Budget	2026 Budget	2027 Budget	2028 Budget	2029 Budget
Agriculture	$ 63,320.23	$ 65,283.57	$ 67,314.28	$ 69,414.46	$ 71,589.28
Commerce	$ 11,325.25	$ 11,676.41	$ 12,039.61	$ 12,415.25	$ 12,804.23
Defense	$ 1,226,315.31	$ 1,270,399.03	$ 1,316,174.34	$ 1,363,710.68	$ 1,413,080.50
Education	$ 539,606.93	$ 561,243.26	$ 583,860.14	$ 607,502.49	$ 632,244.20
Energy	$ 43,422.46	$ 44,768.83	$ 46,161.41	$ 47,601.63	$ 49,093.04
Health and Human Services	$ 1,565,716.02	$ 1,584,160.75	$ 1,598,597.32	$ 1,609,668.15	$ 1,615,488.78
Homeland Security	$ 57,703.18	$ 59,492.34	$ 61,342.92	$ 63,256.79	$ 65,238.69
Housing & Urban Development	$ -	$ -	$ -	$ -	$ -
Interior	$ 16,739.58	$ 17,258.61	$ 17,795.46	$ 18,350.67	$ 18,925.61
Justice	$ 44,084.60	$ 45,451.51	$ 46,865.32	$ 48,327.50	$ 49,841.65
Labor	$ 104,968.30	$ 108,222.98	$ 111,589.38	$ 115,070.92	$ 118,676.20
State	$ 52,054.50	$ 53,668.52	$ 55,337.94	$ 57,064.46	$ 58,852.34
Transportation	$ 108,563.59	$ 111,929.75	$ 115,411.44	$ 119,012.24	$ 122,741.00
Treasury	$ 18,926.88	$ 19,513.73	$ 20,120.73	$ 20,748.49	$ 21,398.56
Veterans	$ 125,200.86	$ 129,082.89	$ 133,098.15	$ 137,250.76	$ 141,550.96
Army Corps of Engineers	$ 9,299.76	$ 9,588.12	$ 9,886.36	$ 10,194.82	$ 10,514.23
Environmental Protection Agency	$ 16,739.58	$ 17,258.61	$ 17,795.46	$ 18,350.67	$ 18,925.61
NASA	$ 37,199.06	$ 38,352.46	$ 39,545.46	$ 40,779.26	$ 42,056.91
National Science Foundation	$ 11,159.72	$ 11,505.74	$ 11,863.64	$ 12,233.78	$ 12,617.07
Small Business Administration	$ 1,270.35	$ 1,309.74	$ 1,350.48	$ 1,392.61	$ 1,436.24
Social Security Administration	$ 1,929,153.92	$ 1,948,926.25	$ 1,962,557.89	$ 1,971,015.03	$ 1,971,454.60
Total	**$ 5,982,770**	**$ 6,109,093**	**$ 6,228,708**	**$ 6,343,361**	**$ 6,448,530**
Interest on National Debt	$ 205,449.56	$ 214,852.59	$ 220,159.64	$ 220,557.52	$ 216,000.00
Total Outlays	*$ 6,188,219.62*	*$ 6,323,945.70*	*$ 6,448,867.37*	*$ 6,563,918.17*	*$ 6,664,529.69*
Tax Base	**$ 10,343,299.46**	**$ 10,757,031.44**	**$ 11,187,312.70**	**$ 11,634,805.20**	**$ 12,100,197.41**
Tax Rate	67%	67%	67%	67%	67%
Gross Sales Tax Receipts	$ 6,895,533.32	$ 7,171,354.65	$ 7,458,208.84	$ 7,756,537.19	$ 8,066,798.68
Non Compliance at 13%	$ (896,419.33)	$ (932,276.10)	$ (969,567.15)	$ (1,008,349.83)	$ (1,048,683.83)
State Collection Fees at 1%	$ (68,955.33)	$ (71,713.55)	$ (74,582.09)	$ (77,565.37)	$ (80,667.99)
Retailer Collection Fees at 1%	$ (68,955.33)	$ (71,713.55)	$ (74,582.09)	$ (77,565.37)	$ (80,667.99)
Customs Revenue	$ 45,970.22	$ 47,809.03	$ 49,721.39	$ 51,710.25	$ 53,778.66
Other Revenue	$ 45,970.22	$ 47,809.03	$ 49,721.39	$ 51,710.25	$ 53,778.66
Total Receipts	*$ 5,953,143.76*	*$ 6,191,269.51*	*$ 6,438,920.29*	*$ 6,696,477.10*	*$ 6,964,336.19*
Surplus (Deficit)	**$ (235,075.86)**	**$ (132,676.18)**	**$ (9,947.08)**	**$ 132,558.93**	**$ 299,806.50**
Debt Retirement	$ -	$ -	$ -	$ 113,938.08	$ 300,000.00
Debt	*$ 5,371,314.82*	*$ 5,503,991.00*	*$ 5,513,938.08*	*$ 5,400,000.00*	*$ 5,100,000.00*
Cumulative Reserve	*$ -*	*$ -*	*$ -*	*$ 8,673.77*	*$ 8,480.27*

PROJECTED US GOVERNMENT BUDGETS
2005 - 2079
(All figures in millions)

Department	2030 Budget	2031 Budget	2032 Budget	2033 Budget	2034 Budget
Agriculture	$ 73,842.12	$ 76,176.05	$ 78,596.97	$ 81,110.48	$ 83,723.05
Commerce	$ 13,207.16	$ 13,624.60	$ 14,057.60	$ 14,507.16	$ 14,974.43
Defense	$ 1,464,359.41	$ 1,517,626.34	$ 1,572,963.69	$ 1,630,457.48	$ 1,690,197.50
Education	$ 658,145.77	$ 685,266.98	$ 713,695.58	$ 743,519.72	$ 774,838.81
Energy	$ 50,637.95	$ 52,238.46	$ 53,898.63	$ 55,622.29	$ 57,413.88
Health and Human Services	$ 1,616,162.13	$ 1,612,225.81	$ 1,602,397.27	$ 1,586,185.95	$ 1,563,069.12
Homeland Security	$ 67,291.68	$ 69,418.57	$ 71,624.74	$ 73,915.26	$ 76,296.08
Housing & Urban Development	$ -	$ -	$ -	$ -	$ -
Interior	$ 19,521.18	$ 20,138.19	$ 20,778.19	$ 21,442.67	$ 22,133.34
Justice	$ 51,410.12	$ 53,035.04	$ 54,720.52	$ 56,470.47	$ 58,289.38
Labor	$ 122,410.82	$ 126,279.87	$ 130,293.11	$ 134,459.85	$ 138,790.80
State	$ 60,704.37	$ 62,623.05	$ 64,613.25	$ 66,679.56	$ 68,827.31
Transportation	$ 126,603.54	$ 130,605.10	$ 134,755.81	$ 139,065.26	$ 143,544.55
Treasury	$ 22,071.95	$ 22,769.58	$ 23,493.21	$ 24,244.52	$ 25,025.43
Veterans	$ 146,005.43	$ 150,620.22	$ 155,407.02	$ 160,376.90	$ 165,542.63
Army Corps of Engineers	$ 10,845.10	$ 11,187.88	$ 11,543.44	$ 11,912.60	$ 12,296.30
Environmental Protection Agency	$ 19,521.18	$ 20,138.19	$ 20,778.19	$ 21,442.67	$ 22,133.34
NASA	$ 43,380.40	$ 44,751.53	$ 46,173.76	$ 47,650.38	$ 49,185.20
National Science Foundation	$ 13,014.12	$ 13,425.46	$ 13,852.13	$ 14,295.12	$ 14,755.56
Small Business Administration	$ 1,481.44	$ 1,526.26	$ 1,576.83	$ 1,627.26	$ 1,679.67
Social Security Administration	$ 1,964,027.43	$ 1,949,539.42	$ 1,926,049.89	$ 1,892,809.87	$ 1,849,018.72
Total	**$ 6,544,643**	**$ 6,633,219**	**$ 6,711,270**	**$ 6,777,795**	**$ 6,831,735**
Interest on National Debt	$ 204,000.00	$ 184,000.00	$ 156,000.00	$ 118,000.00	$ 68,000.00
Total Outlays	***$ 6,748,643.31***	***$ 6,817,218.60***	***$ 6,867,269.84***	***$ 6,895,795.50***	***$ 6,899,735.12***
Tax Base	**$ 12,584,205.31**	**$ 13,087,573.52**	**$ 13,611,076.46**	**$ 14,155,519.52**	**$ 14,721,740.30**
Tax Rate	67%	67%	67%	67%	67%
Gross Sales Tax Receipts	**$ 8,389,470.63**	**$ 8,725,049.45**	**$ 9,074,051.43**	**$ 9,437,013.49**	**$ 9,814,494.02**
Non Compliance at 13%	$ (1,090,631.18)	$ (1,134,256.43)	$ (1,179,626.69)	$ (1,226,811.75)	$ (1,275,884.22)
State Collection Fees at 1%	$ (83,894.71)	$ (87,250.49)	$ (90,740.51)	$ (94,370.13)	$ (98,144.94)
Retailer Collection Fees at 1%	$ (83,894.71)	$ (87,250.49)	$ (90,740.51)	$ (94,370.13)	$ (98,144.94)
Customs Revenue	$ 55,929.80	$ 58,166.99	$ 60,493.67	$ 62,913.42	$ 65,429.96
Other Revenue	$ 55,929.80	$ 58,166.99	$ 60,493.67	$ 62,913.42	$ 65,429.96
Total Receipts	***$ 7,242,909.63***	***$ 7,532,626.02***	***$ 7,833,931.06***	***$ 8,147,288.30***	***$ 8,473,179.83***
Surplus (Deficit)	**$ 494,266.32**	**$ 715,407.42**	**$ 966,661.22**	**$ 1,251,492.81**	**$ 1,573,444.71**
Debt Retirement	$ 500,000.00	$ 700,000.00	$ 950,000.00	$ 1,250,000.00	$ 1,500,000.00
Debt	***$ 4,600,000.00***	***$ 3,900,000.00***	***$ 2,950,000.00***	***$ 1,700,000.00***	***$ 200,000.00***
Cumulative Reserve	***$ 2,746.59***	***$ 18,154.01***	***$ 34,815.23***	***$ 36,308.04***	***$ 109,752.75***

PROJECTED US GOVERNMENT BUDGETS
2005 - 2079
(All figures in millions)

Department	2035 Budget	2036 Budget	2037 Budget	2038 Budget	2039 Budget
Agriculture	$ 86,442.24	$ 89,235.96	$ 92,150.34	$ 95,243.80	$ 98,441.68
Commerce	$ 15,460.78	$ 15,960.46	$ 16,481.71	$ 17,035.00	$ 17,606.96
Defense	$ 1,752,277.54	$ 1,816,795.50	$ 1,883,853.66	$ 1,953,558.81	$ 2,026,022.51
Education	$ 807,766.25	$ 842,045.46	$ 878,154.77	$ 916,709.84	$ 957,057.16
Energy	$ 59,278.60	$ 61,194.42	$ 63,192.98	$ 65,314.35	$ 67,507.33
Health and Human Services	$ 1,532,488.88	$ 1,513,401.52	$ 1,484,519.08	$ 1,426,603.23	$ 1,376,213.49
Homeland Security	$ 78,774.06	$ 81,319.95	$ 83,975.80	$ 86,794.84	$ 89,709.05
Housing & Urban Development	$ -	$ -	$ -	$ -	$ -
Interior	$ 22,852.20	$ 23,590.76	$ 24,361.21	$ 25,179.01	$ 26,024.41
Justice	$ 60,182.53	$ 62,127.56	$ 64,156.60	$ 66,310.32	$ 68,536.74
Labor	$ 143,298.50	$ 147,929.76	$ 152,761.03	$ 157,889.17	$ 163,190.43
State	$ 71,062.71	$ 73,359.38	$ 75,755.25	$ 78,298.32	$ 80,927.25
Transportation	$ 148,206.65	$ 152,996.53	$ 157,993.28	$ 163,297.06	$ 168,779.89
Treasury	$ 25,838.22	$ 26,673.28	$ 27,544.41	$ 28,469.07	$ 29,424.94
Veterans	$ 170,919.19	$ 176,443.12	$ 182,205.62	$ 188,322.20	$ 194,645.27
Army Corps of Engineers	$ 12,695.66	$ 13,105.98	$ 13,534.01	$ 13,988.34	$ 14,458.01
Environmental Protection Agency	$ 22,852.20	$ 23,590.76	$ 24,361.21	$ 25,179.01	$ 26,024.41
NASA	$ 50,782.66	$ 52,423.90	$ 54,136.02	$ 55,953.35	$ 57,832.03
National Science Foundation	$ 15,234.80	$ 15,727.17	$ 16,240.81	$ 16,786.01	$ 17,349.61
Small Business Administration	$ 1,734.23	$ 1,790.28	$ 1,848.75	$ 1,910.81	$ 1,974.96
Social Security Administration	$ 1,793,818.63	$ 1,755,854.02	$ 1,702,948.27	$ 1,605,944.69	$ 1,520,137.24
Total	**$ 6,871,966**	**$ 6,945,566**	**$ 7,000,175**	**$ 6,988,787**	**$ 7,001,863**
Interest on National Debt	$ 8,000.00	$ -	$ -	$ -	$ -
Total Outlays	***$ 6,879,966.50***	***$ 6,945,565.78***	***$ 7,000,174.81***	***$ 6,988,787.21***	***$ 7,001,863.38***
Tax Base	**$ 15,310,609.91**	**$ 15,923,034.31**	**$ 16,559,955.68**	**$ 17,222,353.91**	**$ 17,911,248.07**
Tax Rate	**57%**	**54%**	**51%**	**48%**	**45%**
Gross Sales Tax Receipts	**$ 8,727,047.65**	**$ 8,598,438.53**	**$ 8,445,577.40**	**$ 8,266,729.88**	**$ 8,060,061.63**
Non Compliance at 13%	$ (1,134,516.19)	$ (1,117,797.01)	$ (1,097,925.06)	$ (1,074,674.88)	$ (1,047,808.01)
State Collection Fees at 1%	$ (87,270.48)	$ (85,984.39)	$ (84,455.77)	$ (82,667.30)	$ (80,600.62)
Retailer Collection Fees at 1%	$ (87,270.48)	$ (85,984.39)	$ (84,455.77)	$ (82,667.30)	$ (80,600.62)
Customs Revenue	$ 68,047.16	$ 70,769.04	$ 73,599.80	$ 76,543.80	$ 79,605.55
Other Revenue	$ 68,047.16	$ 70,769.04	$ 73,599.80	$ 76,543.80	$ 79,605.55
Total Receipts	***$ 7,554,084.81***	***$ 7,450,210.83***	***$ 7,325,940.39***	***$ 7,179,807.99***	***$ 7,010,263.48***
Surplus (Deficit)	**$ 674,118.32**	**$ 504,645.05**	**$ 325,765.59**	**$ 191,020.78**	**$ 8,400.10**
Debt Retirement	$ 200,000.00	$ -	$ -	$ -	$ -
Debt	***$ -***	***$ -***	***$ -***	***$ -***	***$ -***
Cumulative Reserve	***$ 583,871.07***	***$ 1,088,516.12***	***$ 1,414,281.71***	***$ 1,605,302.48***	***$ 1,613,702.58***

PROJECTED US GOVERNMENT BUDGETS
2005 - 2079
(All figures in millions)

Department	2040 Budget	2041 Budget	2042 Budget	2043 Budget	2044 Budget
Agriculture	$ 101,806.75	$ 105,190.99	$ 108,716.80	$ 112,419.08	$ 116,260.17
Commerce	$ 18,208.83	$ 18,814.12	$ 19,444.74	$ 20,106.91	$ 20,793.92
Defense	$ 2,101,361.27	$ 2,179,696.84	$ 2,261,156.39	$ 2,345,872.80	$ 2,433,984.92
Education	$ 999,865.56	$ 1,043,740.00	$ 1,089,937.71	$ 1,138,882.15	$ 1,190,271.00
Energy	$ 69,814.96	$ 72,135.73	$ 74,553.59	$ 77,092.46	$ 79,726.53
Health and Human Services	$ 1,313,374.98	$ 1,285,598.33	$ 1,253,538.40	$ 1,210,990.72	$ 1,170,108.94
Homeland Security	$ 92,775.60	$ 95,859.63	$ 99,072.67	$ 102,446.53	$ 105,946.88
Housing & Urban Development	$ -	$ -	$ -	$ -	$ -
Interior	$ 26,914.02	$ 27,808.69	$ 28,740.78	$ 29,719.53	$ 30,734.98
Justice	$ 70,879.55	$ 73,235.72	$ 75,690.44	$ 78,268.04	$ 80,942.27
Labor	$ 168,768.82	$ 174,379.00	$ 180,223.86	$ 186,361.27	$ 192,728.79
State	$ 83,693.62	$ 86,475.74	$ 89,374.25	$ 92,417.84	$ 95,575.53
Transportation	$ 174,549.35	$ 180,351.69	$ 186,396.74	$ 192,744.37	$ 199,329.98
Treasury	$ 30,430.78	$ 31,442.35	$ 32,496.24	$ 33,602.88	$ 34,751.01
Veterans	$ 201,298.89	$ 207,990.43	$ 214,961.88	$ 222,282.28	$ 229,877.13
Army Corps of Engineers	$ 14,952.23	$ 15,449.27	$ 15,967.10	$ 16,510.85	$ 17,074.99
Environmental Protection Agency	$ 26,914.02	$ 27,808.69	$ 28,740.78	$ 29,719.53	$ 30,734.98
NASA	$ 59,808.92	$ 61,797.08	$ 63,868.40	$ 66,043.40	$ 68,299.95
National Science Foundation	$ 17,942.68	$ 18,539.12	$ 19,160.52	$ 19,813.02	$ 20,489.98
Small Business Administration	$ 2,042.47	$ 2,110.37	$ 2,181.11	$ 2,255.38	$ 2,332.44
Social Security Administration	$ 1,415,246.19	$ 1,363,371.71	$ 1,304,852.78	$ 1,230,233.86	$ 1,157,980.38
Total	**$ 6,990,649**	**$ 7,071,796**	**$ 7,149,075**	**$ 7,207,783**	**$ 7,277,945**
Interest on National Debt	$ -	$ -	$ -	$ -	$ -
Total Outlays	**$ 6,990,649.48**	**$ 7,071,795.52**	**$ 7,149,075.20**	**$ 7,207,782.91**	**$ 7,277,944.74**
Tax Base	**$ 18,627,697.99**	**$ 19,372,805.91**	**$ 20,147,718.14**	**$ 20,953,626.87**	**$ 21,791,771.95**
Tax Rate	**42%**	**41%**	**40%**	**39%**	**38**
Gross Sales Tax Receipts	$ 7,823,633.16	$ 7,942,850.42	$ 8,059,087.26	$ 8,171,914.48	$ 8,280,873.34
Non Compliance at 13%	$ (1,017,072.31)	$ (1,032,570.55)	$ (1,047,681.34)	$ (1,062,348.88)	$ (1,076,513.53)
State Collection Fees at 1%	$ (78,236.33)	$ (79,428.50)	$ (80,590.87)	$ (81,719.14)	$ (82,808.73)
Retailer Collection Fees at 1%	$ (78,236.33)	$ (79,428.50)	$ (80,590.87)	$ (81,719.14)	$ (82,808.73)
Customs Revenue	$ 82,789.77	$ 86,101.36	$ 89,545.41	$ 93,127.23	$ 96,852.32
Other Revenue	$ 82,789.77	$ 86,101.36	$ 89,545.41	$ 93,127.23	$ 96,852.32
Total Receipts	**$ 6,815,667.72**	**$ 6,923,625.58**	**$ 7,029,315.00**	**$ 7,132,381.77**	**$ 7,232,446.98**
Surplus (Deficit)	$ (174,981.76)	$ (148,169.94)	$ (119,760.20)	$ (75,401.14)	$ (45,497.76)
Debt Retirement	$ -	$ -	$ -	$ -	$ -
Debt	$ -	$ -	$ -	$ -	$ -
Cumulative Reserve	**$ 1,438,720.82**	**$ 1,290,550.88**	**$ 1,170,790.68**	**$ 1,095,389.54**	**$ 1,049,891.78**

PROJECTED US GOVERNMENT BUDGETS
2005 - 2079
(All figures in millions)

Department	2045 Budget	2046 Budget	2047 Budget	2048 Budget	2049 Budget
Agriculture	$ 120,277.96	$ 124,493.45	$ 128,920.03	$ 133,599.99	$ 138,517.88
Commerce	$ 21,512.53	$ 22,266.50	$ 23,058.22	$ 23,895.26	$ 24,774.86
Defense	$ 2,525,637.84	$ 2,620,983.19	$ 2,720,179.47	$ 2,823,392.31	$ 2,930,794.87
Education	$ 1,244,570.50	$ 1,302,089.24	$ 1,363,068.71	$ 1,426,068.40	$ 1,497,047.95
Energy	$ 82,481.77	$ 85,372.58	$ 88,408.15	$ 91,617.48	$ 94,989.97
Health and Human Services	$ 1,124,139.44	$ 1,071,777.81	$ 1,013,739.15	$ 946,627.71	$ 876,355.30
Homeland Security	$ 109,608.26	$ 113,449.79	$ 117,483.70	$ 121,748.51	$ 126,230.13
Housing & Urban Development	$ -	$ -	$ -	$ -	$ -
Interior	$ 31,797.14	$ 32,911.56	$ 34,081.79	$ 35,319.00	$ 36,619.11
Justice	$ 83,739.52	$ 86,674.41	$ 89,756.28	$ 93,014.54	$ 96,438.45
Labor	$ 199,389.24	$ 206,377.40	$ 213,715.52	$ 221,473.66	$ 229,626.22
State	$ 98,876.49	$ 102,343.97	$ 105,982.99	$ 109,830.31	$ 113,873.22
Transportation	$ 206,218.56	$ 213,446.07	$ 221,035.53	$ 229,059.39	$ 237,491.19
Treasury	$ 35,951.96	$ 37,212.00	$ 38,535.14	$ 39,934.01	$ 41,404.00
Veterans	$ 237,821.38	$ 246,156.50	$ 254,909.03	$ 264,162.55	$ 273,886.51
Army Corps of Engineers	$ 17,665.08	$ 18,284.20	$ 18,934.33	$ 19,621.67	$ 20,343.95
Environmental Protection Agency	$ 31,797.14	$ 32,911.56	$ 34,081.79	$ 35,319.00	$ 36,619.11
NASA	$ 70,660.30	$ 73,136.79	$ 75,737.30	$ 78,486.66	$ 81,375.80
National Science Foundation	$ 21,198.09	$ 21,941.04	$ 22,721.19	$ 23,546.00	$ 24,412.74
Small Business Administration	$ 2,413.05	$ 2,497.62	$ 2,586.43	$ 2,680.32	$ 2,778.98
Social Security Administration	$ 1,077,802.77	$ 987,681.46	$ 888,669.71	$ 775,519.61	$ 657,231.68
Total	**$ 7,343,561**	**$ 7,402,007**	**$ 7,455,604**	**$ 7,496,916**	**$ 7,540,812**
Interest on National Debt	$ -	$ -	$ -	$ -	$ -
Total Outlays	*$ 7,343,560.99*	*$ 7,402,007.11*	*$ 7,455,604.44*	*$ 7,496,916.38*	*$ 7,540,811.91*
Tax Base	**$ 22,663,442.82**	**$ 23,569,980.54**	**$ 24,512,779.76**	**$ 25,493,290.95**	**$ 26,513,022.59**
Tax Rate	37%	36%	35%	34%	33%
Gross Sales Tax Receipts	$ 8,385,473.84	$ 8,485,192.99	$ 8,579,472.92	$ 8,667,718.92	$ 8,749,297.45
Non Compliance at 13%	$ (1,090,111.60)	$ (1,103,075.09)	$ (1,115,331.48)	$ (1,126,803.46)	$ (1,137,408.67)
State Collection Fees at 1%	$ (83,854.74)	$ (84,851.93)	$ (85,794.73)	$ (86,677.19)	$ (87,492.97)
Retailer Collection Fees at 1%	$ (83,854.74)	$ (84,851.93)	$ (85,794.73)	$ (86,677.19)	$ (87,492.97)
Customs Revenue	$ 100,726.41	$ 104,755.47	$ 108,945.69	$ 113,303.52	$ 117,835.66
Other Revenue	$ 100,726.41	$ 104,755.47	$ 108,945.69	$ 113,303.52	$ 117,835.66
Total Receipts	*$ 7,329,105.59*	*$ 7,421,924.98*	*$ 7,510,443.35*	*$ 7,594,168.11*	*$ 7,672,574.15*
Surplus (Deficit)	$ (14,455.40)	$ 19,917.87	$ 54,838.92	$ 97,251.73	$ 131,762.24
Debt Retirement	$ -	$ -	$ -	$ -	$ -
Debt	$ -	$ -	$ -	$ -	$ -
Cumulative Reserve	*$ 1,035,436.38*	*$ 1,055,354.25*	*$ 1,110,193.16*	*$ 1,207,444.90*	*$ 1,339,207.14*

PROJECTED US GOVERNMENT BUDGETS
2005 - 2079
(All figures in millions)

Department	2050 Budget	2051 Budget	2052 Budget	2053 Budget	2054 Budget
Agriculture	$ 143,726.50	$ 149,257.98	$ 155,173.81	$ 160,211.90	$ 165,418.63
Commerce	$ 25,706.46	$ 26,695.80	$ 27,753.89	$ 28,654.98	$ 29,586.24
Defense	$ 3,042,568.17	$ 3,158,901.45	$ 3,279,992.57	$ 3,406,048.43	$ 3,537,285.36
Education	$ 1,570,710.08	$ 1,649,559.13	$ 1,734,449.70	$ 1,811,309.40	$ 1,891,813.84
Energy	$ 98,561.83	$ 102,355.09	$ 106,411.93	$ 109,866.85	$ 113,437.41
Health and Human Services	$ 798,983.66	$ 714,636.96	$ 621,237.60	$ 632,867.31	$ 644,617.06
Homeland Security	$ 130,976.71	$ 136,017.49	$ 141,408.54	$ 145,999.71	$ 150,744.55
Housing & Urban Development	$ -	$ -	$ -	$ -	$ -
Interior	$ 37,996.08	$ 39,458.40	$ 41,022.33	$ 42,354.22	$ 43,730.69
Justice	$ 100,064.79	$ 103,915.89	$ 108,034.59	$ 111,542.19	$ 115,167.20
Labor	$ 238,260.75	$ 247,430.48	$ 257,237.38	$ 265,589.20	$ 274,220.59
State	$ 118,155.14	$ 122,702.47	$ 127,565.78	$ 131,707.51	$ 135,987.87
Transportation	$ 246,421.46	$ 255,905.26	$ 266,048.06	$ 274,685.95	$ 283,612.97
Treasury	$ 42,960.90	$ 44,614.30	$ 46,382.58	$ 47,888.51	$ 49,444.83
Veterans	$ 284,185.34	$ 295,122.53	$ 306,819.71	$ 316,781.34	$ 327,076.42
Army Corps of Engineers	$ 21,108.93	$ 21,921.33	$ 22,790.19	$ 23,530.12	$ 24,294.83
Environmental Protection Agency	$ 37,996.08	$ 39,458.40	$ 41,022.33	$ 42,354.22	$ 43,730.69
NASA	$ 84,435.73	$ 87,685.33	$ 91,160.74	$ 94,120.49	$ 97,179.31
National Science Foundation	$ 25,330.72	$ 26,305.60	$ 27,348.22	$ 28,236.15	$ 29,153.79
Small Business Administration	$ 2,883.48	$ 2,994.45	$ 3,113.14	$ 3,214.21	$ 3,318.67
Social Security Administration	$ 527,707.90	$ 387,055.46	$ 231,956.33	$ 227,512.97	$ 222,543.40
Total	**$ 7,578,741**	**$ 7,611,994**	**$ 7,636,929**	**$ 7,904,476**	**$ 8,182,364**
Interest on National Debt	$ -	$ -	$ -	$ -	$ -
Total Outlays	***$ 7,578,740.70***	***$ 7,611,993.81***	***$ 7,636,929.44***	***$ 7,904,475.68***	***$ 8,182,364.37***
Tax Base	**$ 27,573,543.49**	**$ 28,676,485.23**	**$ 29,823,544.64**	**$ 31,016,486.42**	**$ 32,257,145.88**
Tax Rate	**32%**	**31%**	**30%**	**29%**	**29%**
Gross Sales Tax Receipts	**$ 8,823,533.92**	**$ 8,889,710.42**	**$ 8,947,063.39**	**$ 8,994,781.06**	**$ 9,354,572.31**
Non Compliance at 13%	$ (1,147,059.41)	$ (1,155,662.35)	$ (1,163,118.24)	$ (1,169,321.54)	$ (1,216,094.40)
State Collection Fees at 1%	$ (88,235.34)	$ (88,897.10)	$ (89,470.63)	$ (89,947.81)	$ (93,545.72)
Retailer Collection Fees at 1%	$ (88,235.34)	$ (88,897.10)	$ (89,470.63)	$ (89,947.81)	$ (93,545.72)
Customs Revenue	$ 122,549.08	$ 127,451.05	$ 132,549.09	$ 137,851.05	$ 143,365.09
Other Revenue	$ 122,549.08	$ 127,451.05	$ 132,549.09	$ 137,851.05	$ 143,365.09
Total Receipts	***$ 7,745,101.99***	***$ 7,811,155.95***	***$ 7,870,102.06***	***$ 7,921,266.00***	***$ 8,238,116.64***
Surplus (Deficit)	**$ 166,361.29**	**$ 199,162.13**	**$ 233,172.62**	**$ 16,790.32**	**$ 55,752.28**
Debt Retirement	$ -	$ -	$ -	$ -	$ -
Debt	*$ -*	*$ -*	*$ -*	*$ -*	*$ -*
Cumulative Reserve	***$ 1,505,568.43***	***$ 1,704,730.57***	***$ 1,937,903.18***	***$ 1,954,693.51***	***$ 2,010,445.79***

PROJECTED US GOVERNMENT BUDGETS
2005 - 2079
(All figures in millions)

Department	55 Budget	2056 Budget	2057 Budget	2058 Budget	2059 Budget
Agriculture	$ 170,794.04	$ 176,350.04	$ 182,092.72	$ 188,028.69	$ 194,169.77
Commerce	$ 30,547.67	$ 31,541.40	$ 32,568.52	$ 33,630.20	$ 34,728.58
Defense	$ 3,673,929.60	$ 3,816,217.77	$ 3,964,397.34	$ 4,118,727.17	$ 4,279,478.03
Education	$ 1,976,078.49	$ 2,064,361.84	$ 2,156,863.72	$ 2,253,798.33	$ 2,355,451.48
Energy	$ 117,123.65	$ 120,933.74	$ 124,871.83	$ 128,942.48	$ 133,153.79
Health and Human Services	$ 657,735.91	$ 670,876.00	$ 684,057.21	$ 697,226.53	$ 709,309.00
Homeland Security	$ 155,643.11	$ 160,706.25	$ 165,939.51	$ 171,348.90	$ 176,945.22
Housing & Urban Development	$ -	$ -	$ -	$ -	$ -
Interior	$ 45,151.75	$ 46,620.56	$ 48,138.72	$ 49,707.97	$ 51,331.45
Justice	$ 118,909.65	$ 122,777.84	$ 126,775.99	$ 130,908.71	$ 135,184.23
Labor	$ 283,131.60	$ 292,342.00	$ 301,861.85	$ 311,702.12	$ 321,882.43
State	$ 140,406.90	$ 144,974.41	$ 149,695.36	$ 154,575.22	$ 159,623.71
Transportation	$ 292,829.19	$ 302,355.06	$ 312,200.98	$ 322,378.29	$ 332,907.28
Treasury	$ 51,051.58	$ 52,712.31	$ 54,428.64	$ 56,203.15	$ 58,038.76
Veterans	$ 337,705.02	$ 348,690.72	$ 360,045.51	$ 371,782.49	$ 383,925.04
Army Corps of Engineers	$ 25,084.31	$ 25,900.31	$ 26,743.73	$ 27,615.54	$ 28,517.47
Environmental Protection Agency	$ 45,151.75	$ 46,620.56	$ 48,138.72	$ 49,707.97	$ 51,331.45
NASA	$ 100,337.23	$ 103,601.25	$ 106,974.93	$ 110,462.16	$ 114,069.89
National Science Foundation	$ 30,101.17	$ 31,080.37	$ 32,092.48	$ 33,138.65	$ 34,220.97
Small Business Administration	$ 3,426.52	$ 3,537.98	$ 3,653.19	$ 3,772.28	$ 3,895.49
Social Security Administration	$ 217,009.83	$ 210,888.72	$ 204,146.36	$ 196,747.83	$ 188,661.28
Total	**$ 8,472,149**	**$ 8,773,089**	**$ 9,085,688**	**$ 9,410,405**	**$ 9,746,825**
Interest on National Debt	$ -	$ -	$ -	$ -	$ -
Total Outlays	*$ 8,472,149*	*$ 8,773,089*	*$ 9,085,688*	*$ 9,410,405*	*$ 9,746,825*
Tax Base	**$ 33,547,431.72**	**$ 34,889,328.98**	**$ 36,284,902.14**	**$ 37,736,298.23**	**$ 39,245,750.16**
Tax Rate	**29%**	**29%**	**29%**	**29%**	**29%**
Gross Sales Tax Receipts	**$ 9,728,755.20**	**$ 10,117,905.41**	**$ 10,522,621.62**	**$ 10,943,526.49**	**$ 11,381,267.55**
Non Compliance at 13%	$ (1,264,738.18)	$ (1,315,327.70)	$ (1,367,940.81)	$ (1,422,658.44)	$ (1,479,564.78)
State Collection Fees at 1%	$ (97,287.55)	$ (101,179.05)	$ (105,226.22)	$ (109,435.26)	$ (113,812.68)
Retailer Collection Fees at 1%	$ (97,287.55)	$ (101,179.05)	$ (105,226.22)	$ (109,435.26)	$ (113,812.68)
Customs Revenue	$ 149,099.70	$ 155,063.68	$ 161,266.23	$ 167,716.88	$ 174,425.56
Other Revenue	$ 149,099.70	$ 155,063.68	$ 161,266.23	$ 167,716.88	$ 174,425.56
Total Receipts	*$ 8,567,641.31*	*$ 8,910,346.96*	*$ 9,266,760.84*	*$ 9,637,431.28*	*$10,022,928.53*
Surplus (Deficit)	**$ 95,492.32**	**$ 137,257.83**	**$ 181,073.32**	**$ 227,026.58**	**$ 276,103.21**
Debt Retirement	$ -	$ -	$ -	$ -	$ -
Debt	*$ -*	*$ -*	*$ -*	*$ -*	*$ -*
Cumulative Reserve	*$ 2,105,938.11*	*$ 2,243,195.94*	*$ 2,424,269.26*	*$ 2,651,295.83*	*$ 2,927,399.04*

PROJECTED US GOVERNMENT BUDGETS
2005 - 2079
(All figures in millions)

Department	2060 Budget	2061 Budget	2062 Budget	2063 Budget	2064 Budget
Agriculture	$ 200,512.17	$ 207,068.55	$ 213,849.28	$ 220,858.66	$ 228,105.81
Commerce	$ 35,862.96	$ 37,035.61	$ 38,248.39	$ 39,502.07	$ 40,798.27
Defense	$ 4,446,933.18	$ 4,621,388.96	$ 4,803,155.44	$ 4,992,557.02	$ 5,189,933.19
Education	$ 2,461,928.86	$ 2,573,543.84	$ 2,690,593.83	$ 2,813,311.32	$ 2,941,999.36
Energy	$ 137,503.15	$ 141,999.25	$ 146,649.20	$ 151,455.95	$ 156,425.75
Health and Human Services	$ 722,496.97	$ 735,617.20	$ 748,064.65	$ 760,482.78	$ 772,614.16
Homeland Security	$ 182,724.99	$ 188,699.76	$ 194,878.98	$ 201,286.57	$ 207,870.83
Housing & Urban Development	$ -	$ -	$ -	$ -	$ -
Interior	$ 53,008.15	$ 54,741.42	$ 56,534.00	$ 58,387.03	$ 60,302.91
Justice	$ 139,599.91	$ 144,164.57	$ 148,885.43	$ 153,765.48	$ 158,811.06
Labor	$ 332,396.45	$ 343,265.21	$ 354,505.87	$ 366,125.59	$ 378,139.45
State	$ 164,837.68	$ 170,227.57	$ 175,801.89	$ 181,564.19	$ 187,521.95
Transportation	$ 343,781.42	$ 355,022.45	$ 366,648.11	$ 378,665.82	$ 391,091.17
Treasury	$ 59,934.55	$ 61,894.30	$ 63,921.11	$ 66,016.27	$ 68,182.49
Veterans	$ 396,465.64	$ 409,429.34	$ 422,836.63	$ 436,696.04	$ 451,025.57
Army Corps of Engineers	$ 29,448.97	$ 30,411.90	$ 31,407.78	$ 32,437.24	$ 33,501.62
Environmental Protection Agency	$ 53,008.15	$ 54,741.42	$ 56,534.00	$ 58,387.03	$ 60,302.91
NASA	$ 117,795.89	$ 121,647.60	$ 125,631.11	$ 129,748.95	$ 134,006.47
National Science Foundation	$ 35,338.77	$ 36,494.28	$ 37,689.33	$ 38,924.68	$ 40,201.94
Small Business Administration	$ 4,022.73	$ 4,154.27	$ 4,290.30	$ 4,430.93	$ 4,576.32
Social Security Administration	$ 179,837.30	$ 170,241.18	$ 159,832.68	$ 148,564.40	$ 136,390.50
Total	**$ 10,097,438**	**$ 10,461,789**	**$ 10,839,958**	**$ 11,233,148**	**$ 11,641,802**
Interest on National Debt	$ -	$ -	$ -	$ -	$ -
Total Outlays	*$ 10,097,438*	*$ 10,461,789*	*$ 10,839,958*	*$ 11,233,148*	*$ 11,641,802*
Tax Base	**$ 40,815,580.16**	**$ 42,448,203.37**	**$ 44,146,131.51**	**$ 45,911,976.77**	**$ 47,748,455.84**
Tax Rate	**29%**	**29%**	**29%**	**28%**	**28%**
Gross Sales Tax Receipts	**$ 11,836,518.25**	**$ 12,309,978.98**	**$ 12,802,378.14**	**$ 12,855,353.49**	**$ 13,369,567.63**
Non Compliance at 13%	$ (1,538,747.37)	$ (1,600,297.27)	$ (1,664,309.16)	$ (1,671,195.95)	$ (1,738,043.79)
State Collection Fees at 1%	$ (118,365.18)	$ (123,099.79)	$ (128,023.78)	$ (128,553.53)	$ (133,695.68)
Retailer Collection Fees at 1%	$ (118,365.18)	$ (123,099.79)	$ (128,023.78)	$ (128,553.53)	$ (133,695.68)
Customs Revenue	$ 181,402.58	$ 188,658.68	$ 196,205.03	$ 204,053.23	$ 212,215.36
Other Revenue	$ 181,402.58	$ 188,658.68	$ 196,205.03	$ 204,053.23	$ 212,215.36
Total Receipts	*$10,423,845.67*	*$10,840,799.49*	*$11,274,431.47*	*$11,335,156.93*	*$11,788,563.21*
Surplus (Deficit)	**$ 326,407.77**	**$ 379,010.81**	**$ 434,473.48**	**$ 102,008.92**	**$ 146,761.48**
Debt Retirement	$ -	$ -	$ -	$ -	$ -
Debt	*$ -*	*$ -*	*$ -*	*$ -*	*$ -*
Cumulative Reserve	*$ 3,253,806.81*	*$ 3,632,817.62*	*$ 4,067,291.09*	*$ 4,169,300.01*	*$ 4,316,061.50*

PROJECTED US GOVERNMENT BUDGETS
2005 - 2079
(All figures in millions)

Department	2065 Budget	2066 Budget	2067 Budget	2068 Budget	2069 Budget
Agriculture	$ 235,595.79	$ 243,339.03	$ 251,344.44	$ 259,620.05	$ 268,175.06
Commerce	$ 42,137.90	$ 43,522.83	$ 44,954.66	$ 46,434.81	$ 47,964.93
Defense	$ 5,395,639.17	$ 5,610,046.74	$ 5,833,544.97	$ 6,066,541.11	$ 6,309,461.42
Education	$ 3,076,920.69	$ 3,218,418.85	$ 3,366,831.19	$ 3,522,496.69	$ 3,685,783.73
Energy	$ 161,562.07	$ 166,872.08	$ 172,361.86	$ 178,036.95	$ 183,903.62
Health and Human Services	$ 785,016.69	$ 797,276.87	$ 809,328.04	$ 821,314.11	$ 833,216.25
Homeland Security	$ 214,696.39	$ 221,752.73	$ 229,047.99	$ 236,589.49	$ 244,385.59
Housing & Urban Development	$ -	$ -	$ -	$ -	$ -
Interior	$ 62,282.99	$ 64,330.02	$ 66,446.36	$ 68,634.14	$ 70,895.77
Justice	$ 164,025.71	$ 169,416.69	$ 174,990.19	$ 180,751.81	$ 186,707.95
Labor	$ 390,555.87	$ 403,392.12	$ 416,662.99	$ 430,381.78	$ 444,563.73
State	$ 193,679.34	$ 200,044.92	$ 206,626.04	$ 213,429.28	$ 220,462.21
Transportation	$ 403,932.87	$ 417,208.78	$ 430,934.19	$ 445,122.87	$ 459,790.57
Treasury	$ 70,421.30	$ 72,735.81	$ 75,128.69	$ 77,602.33	$ 80,159.48
Veterans	$ 465,835.24	$ 481,145.67	$ 496,974.49	$ 513,337.57	$ 530,253.09
Army Corps of Engineers	$ 34,601.66	$ 35,738.90	$ 36,914.65	$ 38,130.08	$ 39,386.54
Environmental Protection Agency	$ 62,282.99	$ 64,330.02	$ 66,446.36	$ 68,634.14	$ 70,895.77
NASA	$ 138,406.64	$ 142,955.60	$ 147,658.58	$ 152,520.30	$ 157,546.15
National Science Foundation	$ 41,521.99	$ 42,886.68	$ 44,297.57	$ 45,756.09	$ 47,263.85
Small Business Administration	$ 4,726.59	$ 4,881.93	$ 5,042.54	$ 5,208.57	$ 5,380.20
Social Security Administration	$ 123,260.34	$ 109,124.13	$ 93,928.43	$ 77,616.85	$ 60,130.86
Total	**$ 12,067,102**	**$ 12,509,420**	**$ 12,969,464**	**$ 13,448,159**	**$ 13,946,327**
Interest on National Debt	$ -	$ -	$ -	$ -	$ -
Total Outlays	***$ 12,067,102***	***$ 12,509,420***	***$ 12,969,464***	***$ 13,448,159***	***$ 13,946,327***
Tax Base	**$ 49,658,394.07**	**$ 51,644,729.83**	**$ 53,710,519.03**	**$ 55,858,939.79**	**$ 58,093,297.38**
Tax Rate	**28%**	**28%**	**28%**	**28%**	**28%**
Gross Sales Tax Receipts	**$ 13,904,350.34**	**$ 14,460,524.35**	**$ 15,038,945.33**	**$ 15,640,503.14**	**$ 16,266,123.27**
Non Compliance at 13%	$ (1,807,565.54)	$ (1,879,868.17)	$ (1,955,062.89)	$ (2,033,265.41)	$ (2,114,596.02)
State Collection Fees at 1%	$ (139,043.50)	$ (144,605.24)	$ (150,389.45)	$ (156,405.03)	$ (162,661.23)
Retailer Collection Fees at 1%	$ (139,043.50)	$ (144,605.24)	$ (150,389.45)	$ (156,405.03)	$ (162,661.23)
Customs Revenue	$ 220,703.97	$ 229,532.13	$ 238,713.42	$ 248,261.95	$ 258,192.43
Other Revenue	$ 220,703.97	$ 229,532.13	$ 238,713.42	$ 248,261.95	$ 258,192.43
Total Receipts	***$12,260,105.74***	***$12,750,509.97***	***$13,260,530.36***	***$13,790,951.58***	***$14,342,589.64***
Surplus (Deficit)	**$ 193,003.51**	**$ 241,089.54**	**$ 291,066.12**	**$ 342,792.57**	**$ 396,262.88**
Debt Retirement	$ -	$ -	$ -	$ -	$ -
Debt	***$ -***	***$ -***	***$ -***	***$ -***	***$ -***
Cumulative Reserve	***$ 4,509,065.01***	***$ 4,750,154.55***	***$ 5,041,220.68***	***$ 5,384,013.25***	***$ 5,780,276.13***

PROJECTED US GOVERNMENT BUDGETS
2005 - 2079
(All figures in millions)

Department	2070 Budget	2071 Budget	2072 Budget	2073 Budget	2074 Budget
Agriculture	$ 277,018.81	$ 286,161.16	$ 295,612.23	$ 305,148.71	$ 314,995.77
Commerce	$ 49,546.69	$ 51,181.86	$ 52,872.25	$ 54,577.91	$ 56,339.13
Defense	$ 6,562,752.10	$ 6,826,880.24	$ 7,102,334.85	$ 7,389,627.90	$ 7,689,296.43
Education	$ 3,857,077.75	$ 4,036,787.05	$ 4,225,339.97	$ 4,419,801.37	$ 4,623,655.81
Energy	$ 189,968.31	$ 196,237.76	$ 202,718.93	$ 209,258.66	$ 216,011.38
Health and Human Services	$ 845,038.98	$ 856,748.79	$ 868,324.02	$ 896,336.24	$ 925,260.76
Homeland Security	$ 252,444.82	$ 260,776.17	$ 269,388.84	$ 278,079.35	$ 287,052.90
Housing & Urban Development	$ -	$ -	$ -	$ -	$ -
Interior	$ 73,233.74	$ 75,650.64	$ 78,149.16	$ 80,670.26	$ 83,273.47
Justice	$ 192,865.11	$ 199,230.17	$ 205,810.16	$ 212,449.61	$ 219,305.31
Labor	$ 459,224.34	$ 474,379.96	$ 490,047.35	$ 505,856.32	$ 522,180.16
State	$ 227,732.50	$ 235,248.28	$ 243,017.84	$ 250,857.62	$ 258,952.73
Transportation	$ 474,953.32	$ 490,628.03	$ 506,832.05	$ 523,182.50	$ 540,065.46
Treasury	$ 82,802.94	$ 85,535.66	$ 88,360.65	$ 91,211.18	$ 94,154.54
Veterans	$ 547,739.52	$ 565,816.37	$ 584,503.63	$ 603,359.77	$ 622,830.03
Army Corps of Engineers	$ 40,685.41	$ 42,028.13	$ 43,416.20	$ 44,816.81	$ 46,263.04
Environmental Protection Agency	$ 73,233.74	$ 75,650.64	$ 78,149.16	$ 80,670.26	$ 83,273.47
NASA	$ 162,741.63	$ 168,112.54	$ 173,664.80	$ 179,267.25	$ 185,052.15
National Science Foundation	$ 48,822.49	$ 50,433.76	$ 52,099.44	$ 53,780.17	$ 55,515.65
Small Business Administration	$ 5,557.63	$ 5,741.04	$ 5,930.65	$ 6,121.98	$ 6,319.53
Social Security Administration	$ 41,409.22	$ 21,387.92	$ -	$ -	$ -
Total	**$ 14,464,849**	**$ 15,004,616**	**$ 15,566,572**	**$ 16,185,074**	**$ 16,829,797**
Interest on National Debt	$ -	$ -	$ -	$ -	$ -
Total Outlays	*$ 14,464,849*	*$ 15,004,616*	*$ 15,566,572*	*$ 16,185,074*	*$ 16,829,797*
Tax Base	**$ 60,417,029.27**	**$ 62,833,710.44**	**$ 65,347,058.86**	**$ 67,960,941.22**	**$ 70,679,378.87**
Tax Rate	**28%**	**28%**	**28%**	**27%**	**27%**
Gross Sales Tax Receipts	$ 16,916,768.20	$ 17,593,438.92	$ 18,297,176.48	$ 18,349,454.13	$ 19,083,432.29
Non Compliance at 13%	$ (2,199,179.87)	$ (2,287,147.06)	$ (2,378,632.94)	$ (2,385,429.04)	$ (2,480,846.20)
State Collection Fees at 1%	$ (169,167.68)	$ (175,934.39)	$ (182,971.76)	$ (183,494.54)	$ (190,834.32)
Retailer Collection Fees at 1%	$ (169,167.68)	$ (175,934.39)	$ (182,971.76)	$ (183,494.54)	$ (190,834.32)
Customs Revenue	$ 268,520.13	$ 279,260.94	$ 290,431.37	$ 302,048.63	$ 314,130.57
Other Revenue	$ 268,520.13	$ 279,260.94	$ 290,431.37	$ 302,048.63	$ 314,130.57
Total Receipts	*$14,916,293.23*	*$15,512,944.96*	*$16,133,462.75*	*$16,201,133.26*	*$16,849,178.60*
Surplus (Deficit)	**$ 451,444.19**	**$ 508,328.78**	**$ 566,890.55**	**$ 16,059.39**	**$ 19,381.88**
Debt Retirement	$ -	$ -	$ -	$ -	$ -
Debt	*$ -*	*$ -*	*$ -*	*$ -*	*$ -*
Cumulative Reserve	*$ 6,231,720.31*	*$ 6,740,049.09*	*$ 7,306,939.64*	*$ 7,322,999.03*	*$ 7,342,380.91*

PROJECTED US GOVERNMENT BUDGETS
2005 - 2079
(All figures in millions)

Department	2075 Budget	2076 Budget	2077 Budget	2078 Budget	2079 Budget
Agriculture	$ 325,163.52	$ 335,662.35	$ 346,503.02	$ 357,696.60	$ 369,254.52
Commerce	$ 58,157.70	$ 60,035.49	$ 61,974.41	$ 63,976.46	$ 66,043.67
Defense	$ 8,001,898.71	$ 8,328,025.45	$ 8,668,291.13	$ 9,023,340.29	$ 9,393,847.93
Education	$ 4,837,371.89	$ 5,061,442.01	$ 5,296,383.59	$ 5,542,740.37	$ 5,801,083.73
Energy	$ 222,984.01	$ 230,183.68	$ 237,617.77	$ 245,293.88	$ 253,219.83
Health and Human Services	$ 955,127.25	$ 985,966.26	$ 1,017,809.36	$ 1,050,689.10	$ 1,084,639.05
Homeland Security	$ 296,318.68	$ 305,886.17	$ 315,765.18	$ 325,965.79	$ 336,498.42
Housing & Urban Development	$ -	$ -	$ -	$ -	$ -
Interior	$ 85,961.45	$ 88,736.96	$ 91,602.84	$ 94,562.02	$ 97,617.51
Justice	$ 226,384.26	$ 233,693.72	$ 241,241.17	$ 249,034.33	$ 257,081.15
Labor	$ 539,035.61	$ 556,439.92	$ 574,410.89	$ 592,966.90	$ 612,126.90
State	$ 267,311.46	$ 275,942.38	$ 284,854.31	$ 294,056.36	$ 303,557.93
Transportation	$ 557,498.22	$ 575,498.65	$ 594,085.15	$ 613,276.72	$ 633,092.97
Treasury	$ 97,193.75	$ 100,331.93	$ 103,572.28	$ 106,918.12	$ 110,372.87
Veterans	$ 642,934.35	$ 663,693.33	$ 685,128.19	$ 707,260.86	$ 730,113.93
Army Corps of Engineers	$ 47,756.36	$ 49,298.31	$ 50,890.47	$ 52,534.45	$ 54,231.95
Environmental Protection Agency	$ 85,961.45	$ 88,736.96	$ 91,602.84	$ 94,562.02	$ 97,617.51
NASA	$ 191,025.45	$ 197,193.25	$ 203,561.87	$ 210,137.82	$ 216,927.81
National Science Foundation	$ 57,307.63	$ 59,157.98	$ 61,068.56	$ 63,041.35	$ 65,078.34
Small Business Administration	$ 6,523.52	$ 6,734.15	$ 6,951.64	$ 7,176.21	$ 7,408.08
Social Security Administration	$ -	$ -	$ -	$ -	$ -
Total	$ 17,501,915	$ 18,202,659	$ 18,933,315	$ 19,695,230	$ 20,489,814
Interest on National Debt	$ -	$ -	$ -	$ -	$ -
Total Outlays	*$ 17,501,915*	*$ 18,202,659*	*$ 18,933,315*	*$ 19,695,230*	*$ 20,489,814*
Tax Base	$ 73,506,554.02	$ 76,446,816.18	$ 79,504,688.83	$ 82,684,876.38	$ 85,992,271.44
Tax Rate	27%	27%	27%	27%	27%
Gross Sales Tax Receipts	$ 19,846,769.59	$ 20,640,640.37	$ 21,466,265.98	$ 22,324,916.62	$ 23,217,913.29
Non Compliance at 13%	$ (2,580,080.05)	$ (2,683,283.25)	$ (2,790,614.58)	$ (2,902,239.16)	$ (3,018,328.73)
State Collection Fees at 1%	$ (198,467.70)	$ (206,406.40)	$ (214,662.66)	$ (223,249.17)	$ (232,179.13)
Retailer Collection Fees at 1%	$ (198,467.70)	$ (206,406.40)	$ (214,662.66)	$ (223,249.17)	$ (232,179.13)
Customs Revenue	$ 326,695.80	$ 339,763.63	$ 353,354.17	$ 367,488.34	$ 382,187.87
Other Revenue	$ 326,695.80	$ 339,763.63	$ 353,354.17	$ 367,488.34	$ 382,187.87
Total Receipts	*$17,523,145.74*	*$18,224,071.57*	*$18,953,034.43*	*$19,711,155.81*	*$20,499,602.04*
Surplus (Deficit)	$ 21,230.46	$ 21,412.60	$ 19,719.75	$ 15,926.19	$ 9,787.91
Debt Retirement	$ -	$ -	$ -	$ -	$ -
Debt	*$ -*	*$ -*	*$ -*	*$ -*	*$ -*
Cumulative Reserve	*$ 7,363,611.37*	*$ 7,385,023.97*	*$ 7,404,743.71*	*$ 7,420,669.90*	*$ 7,430,457.82*

"There are different kinds of gifts, but the same Spirit. There are different kinds of service, but the same Lord. There are different kinds of working, but the same God works all of them in all men."
1 Corinthians 12:4-6

CHAPTER FIVE

The 5th Pillar of Freedom: Universal National Service and School Vouchers

Introduction

N ational service and education are combined in the 5th Pillar because they are related: preparation for national service should begin during every student's school years, and some of the structural changes recommended for the government (public) school system will reflect this new emphasis on national service. Likewise, recommendations regarding school vouchers affect both areas, because vouchers will be granted to parents for each of their K-12th graders, and each veteran will receive a school voucher for college level study after successfully completing their required national service.

Background

The current national service situation is unfair—only a small percentage of our young people volunteer to serve in the military or in civilian programs, while everyone benefits. There is no comprehensive mandatory national service policy requiring all young people to sacrifice some of their time for the common good. There is a relationship between mutual sacrifice and mutual ownership in any endeavor, and doing one's part is vital if we believe that "freedom isn't free".

Philosophically I am committed to universal service (all young men and women), thus demonstrating fairness and equality (to the extent that each person's respective gifts, talents, and commitment are utilized appropriately and efficiently). All young Americans should at least be required to serve an equal amount of time, so that national service becomes a societal "right-of-passage" into the full responsibilities, privileges, and rights of adult citizenship.

My call for equal time of service is based on the fact that we all breath the same free air, and no one should be permitted to act as if they were above a reasonable period of required service—to sacrifice in current generations as many of our ancestors did before us— personally investing time and risk to win the comprehensive freedoms we enjoy today.

Now let me be clear: I am not criticizing anyone who had legal options other than the limited national service areas open to young people in previous generations. We have all lived with whatever rules were in place at the time. Even in WWII, only about one third of the sixteen million military personnel who served were volunteers, while the other two-thirds were drafted. And many citizens who were willing to serve were excused from service for a variety of reasons, including key agricultural or industrial jobs, or for medical reasons.

Some family history

The key point is that if you were willing to go and were not drafted, you should not be looked down upon in any way. To illustrate this point, I offer a small snapshot from my own family's history as an example of willingness to serve—yet not all went into the military.

Dr. Michael O. Bentley, the great-grandfather I mentioned earlier volunteered and served in the Civil War, but his son, my grandfather, Edgar Bentley, married relatively young and already had a young son (my father) when the Spanish-American War broke out in 1898. Edgar was living in his home state of New York at the time and would have been more than willing to fight the Spanish in Cuba had he been asked. But he wasn't required to serve and didn't.

By the time my dad, Charles Bentley, graduated from Monterey (California) High School in 1917, World War I was raging and he felt it was his duty to volunteer so he joined the army. He volunteered for the infantry with the thought of heading to France to get into the action, but after an interview at the Presidio of Monterey, he was selected for officer training and sent to U.C. Berkeley's Student Officer Training Corps program (SOTC was a forerunner of current ROTC programs).

Fortunately for him (and me) the war ended a month before he got his commission and accompanying orders to be shipped to France. I say "fortunate" because he'd requested duty as a sapper, and in those days a second lieutenant in a sapper platoon lasted about 5 minutes in combat. With the war over, he was released from service (in those days there was no requirement for the government to continue its commitment to the trainee's education). My dad was offered the opportunity to finish his degree at Cal—but at his own expense. He declined and returned home and joined the family business—a feed store in Seaside, California, owned by his dad. The two of them worked together until my grandfather died in 1934, after which my dad ran the store as a sole proprietor until 1958 when he retired and closed the business.

As for me, I joined the army in 1980 to become a military chaplain. I experienced normal peacetime rotations on active duty and in the National Guard, and I didn't see any combat until 1991 when I volunteered for Desert Storm.

During the war I was assigned to a logistics base in northern Saudi Arabia and did nothing heroic. I watched a B-52 plaster an enemy unit some miles in front of us across the flat desert, and heard the opening volleys from our artillery battalions when they commenced the bombardment of enemy forces the first night of the ground war. But, within hours, the fighting moved away to the north and except for a few scuds that flew overhead, I was never threatened by a shot fired in anger.

Regarding the current generation of adult Bentley's, my older sons were required to register with the Selective Service Agency when they turned eighteen, and they complied as did the majority of their peers. And it is interesting to note that Selective Service reports that about 95% of all young men still comply with the law and register for the draft when they turn 18. This is certainly a good testimony to the patriotism of today's youth. As of the writing of this book, my oldest son has been a soldier for many years (subsequently injured in Afghanistan in 2010 and, fortunately, as of 2012, recovering nicely), and my second son is a youth minister (as of 2012 a high school teacher and football coach).

I include this excerpt from my family history to illustrate the fact that, in the past, varying situations dictated people's entry into national service. Willingness was always the key—but national service has never been universally required or fair.

Our position in the world has changed

As discussed in the 3rd Pillar, America's position in the world has been evolving over the last two century's to the point where we are the world's only super-power. This fact, combined with my philosophical commitment to fairness, are two of the reasons I am calling for a change in our requirement for national service.

Since World War I, U.S. commitment and participation in global conflicts have made the difference in Allied victories, and we really took over leadership of the free world during and after WWII. This trend accelerated during the Cold War as we solidified our role as undisputed leader of the West, a trend that progressed further after the demise of the old Soviet Union in 1990. As a result of this two hundred year evolution, our responsibilities have changed.

As I mentioned in the 3rd Pillar, as a fledging democracy, we had to be inwardly focused to survive (even though we were engaged in international trade and had to fight pirates in distant waters to protect our sailors and sea lanes). But as the centuries passed and we grew stronger, our situational responsibilities progressed accordingly. Today we are the principle hope for oppressed peoples everywhere.

As for the United Nations, I largely discount their usefulness to intimidate dictators who abuse their own people, and have even less hope that this ungainly organization will actually liberate anyone.

The U.N. failed during the Korean War, and even there we led the coalition that carried the brunt of the fighting.

Since the world has come to depend on our proactive leadership, I believe that we should accept our role and help whomever we can. If we can't help in certain situations, Okay. But when we can help and don't, then shame on us. (I give this rather harsh indictment remembering Rwanda, where one million people were massacred. We could have stopped it as we did Saddam's attempt to conquer Saudi Arabia, but we did nothing).

The moral benefits of service

In addition to the international responsibilities mentioned above, I believe it is morally good to require every young person to serve for some reasonable time—I suggest two years. Sacrificing for the good of their fellow citizens will teach each person to respect their heritage—paid for at great cost by those who served in the past. These sacrifices include more than one million military personnel who have died in combat during our 228-year history. It is unhealthy for any culture to have its young people focused only on themselves—sacrificing for the common good teaches responsibility and makes everyone stakeholders.

An equal term of service

Applying our established philosophy of fairness is a vital component of our societal relationships, and we should institute our national service requirements accordingly. Our current national service options, whether in military or civilian sectors, are all truly voluntary, creating a situation where the majority enjoy all the benefits of our free society, but only a minority makes the sacrificial contributions necessary to preserve those benefits.

The service requirements recommended in the 5th Pillar will be a great equalizer, significantly boosting national morale as well as boosting each generation's commitment to our common future. The term of service may be fulfilled in either the military or civilian sectors, but what sets this recommendation apart from previous systems (such as various military drafts implemented in the past) is that everyone at a certain age must step forward and be willing to serve. Impartial testing, individual gifts, and personal desires will be factored into determining what training and assignment each recruit receives—further enhancing the actual and perceived fairness of the new system.

A fair term of national service should contain a time requirement that is predictable, especially in peacetime. Though we are involved in a long-term war against terrorists, by nature it is the kind of lowintensity conflict that is very different from past wars where nations attacked us in force. If such a tragedy occurs in the future, the required term of service could be extended until we achieve victory—plus a reasonable time to consolidate our hard won gains. But we need to bring troops home from a war in the optimum time—meaning neither too soon nor too late. Both of these errors can undermine an effective occupation and/or troop morale.

Currently, if a young person joins the military, he or she must commit to as many as eight years in the active and/or reserve/national guard components. This commitment is too long for most young adults who naturally want to focus on their careers and future family lives. Expecting everyone to serve more than two years after high school is, in most cases, counter-productive and impractical to our goal of giving everyone an opportunity to make a reasonable contribution to the nation—and then get on with their lives. It is reasonable to expect that only a small percentage of citizens desire to make the military a career, and only a third of the force structure I propose will be career professionals (two million military personnel out of six million).

Program specifics

The first component: mandatory national service

I recommend that 95% of MNS trainees serve two years. This reasonable time will be comprised of six months of training and eighteen months of line service. Included in the training phase is three months of basic training (those not assigned to the military will not receive combative instruction unless their follow-on assignments require this knowledge, i.e., some jobs in the Department of Homeland Security). The second three months will be MOS specific (military occupational specialty—what the military member's vocation requires, i.e., infantry versus truck driver versus helicopter mechanic) or civilian-job specific, depending on the requirements of the assigned civilian department.

Those electing to serve in the civilian departments could receive training as teaching assistants (Department of Education), medics (various departments), construction workers (Corps of Engineers), police (Homeland Security), fire fighters and foresters (Interior)—as many areas as are needed and practical for this twoyear commitment.

I have included all of the first six months training costs in the military budget, but each government department may want to establish schools for its own personnel and be granted its portion of the training budget. For ease of calculation I have assigned proportional numbers of personnel and accompanying budget amounts to each federal department based on its percentage of the total budget. This can be changed later according to actual needs of the various agencies, i.e., Homeland Security may need more personnel than their percentage of the total budget, while Agriculture may need fewer personnel.

To keep this national service requirement from being a financial drain on the college and university system who depend on successive classes of freshman to keep the system viable, each school which is willing to receive government funding and maintain ROTC programs will receive financial assistance to get them through this one-time two-year "drought". $10,000 per student has been added to several DOE budgets to compensate the college system for this unusual situation. In 2007, freshmen will again enter college, equipped with significant scholarship financing to help pay for their educations.

The remaining 5% of MNS inductees will make up the majority of young officers, and will receive four-year scholarships in return for attending ROTC programs in the college of their choice (and acceptance). Each of these personnel will be required to serve four years active duty following graduation. Those dropping out of the program after starting, or failing to graduate, will be required to immediately report to their assigned government department to fulfill the normal MNS requirement. They will give one year of service for each year of college started (with a two year minimum like all citizens/permanent residents).

The estimated budget for the ROTC scholarships is $20,000 per student per year for the four years of college. Since these ROTC cadets will attend various colleges with varying tuitions, some scholarships may be higher or lower than the estimated average. Once these ROTC cadets have graduated and received their commissions, the estimated budget for their four years of required service as officers (regardless of where they are assigned throughout various government departments) is $25,000 per officer per year. This is just an estimate: they will be paid whatever junior officers are paid at the time.

This ROTC/officer commitment initially adds $4 billion to the military budget (2005), and increases to a steady state in today's dollars of $36 billion in 2013. The actual figure will be higher at that time due to inflation and cost of living increases (please see the chart and spreadsheets at the end of the chapter).

Students in the 5% category should be selected from the top performers in each high school class (including graduates from government schools, private schools, and home schools). Their selection will be based on grade point average, national test scores, physical fitness requirements, leadership potential, etc., in other words, a formula that determines class standing. Military Academy appointees are relatively few in number (about 3,000 per year) and will not be counted against this total. Any selectee may decline an offered ROTC scholarship and serve the required two years of national service. When a student declines the offer, the next student in line will be offered the ROTC opportunity.

I recommend that each citizen/permanent resident not receive a regular salary during their 2-year service stint (this is sacrificial service for which every MNS will receive training, room, board, etc.). However, I do recommend that everyone who successfully completes his or her service requirement be given a $25,000 education voucher to be used in the higher education institution of their choice (an equivalent to $2,000/month if thought of as compensation). This budget item adds $96 billion to the Department of Education budget beginning in 2007.

From the ranks of Academy, ROTC, and two-year MNS's will come the professional military—those who decide to stay in the service after their MNS commitment is completed. The professional military force structure will grow to approximately 2 million personnel—a base established according to the expanded responsibilities of the military described elsewhere. This number should be as flexible as the mission(s) requirements—military experts may call for a larger force of professionals until the mission of freeing the earth of dangerous dictators, thugs, and terrorists, has been largely completed. At that point we can always reduce the size of our military—perhaps increasing the percentage of MNS personnel who serve in the civilian components of government, particularly in education and medicine.

In summary, millions of young citizens will serve with distinction for succeeding generations, adding their efforts to the tremendous heritage that makes America great. Each citizen will then return to civilian life to pursue whatever career they choose, but will do so having experienced honorable sacrificial service, introductions to possible vocations, a challenging maturing process, and friendships that will last a lifetime.

Do what you can!

It is vital to emphasize that all citizens and permanent residents must serve as best they can. Those with handicaps of various kinds will serve if they are able/as they are able. This is different from the traditional Selective Service approach where a person might have a relatively low-grade abnormality and be excused from military (and all) sacrificial national service. In this new system, everyone serves—but at a level they are able to serve. Some may want to be in the military but don't have the necessary physical attributes—but they may be able to sit at a computer and work for the national weather service, become a teaching assistant, transportation analyst, intelligence agency analyst, medical orderly in a convalescent or VA hospital, etc. **Willingness is the key to successfully completing the requirement.**

Penalties for non-compliance

Unfortunately, there will be a few citizens who shirk their duty and try to weasel out of the new requirements. For those the penalty will be severe: They will not receive the post-service education voucher, nor will they be eligible for admittance to any college that receives government funds. They will not be permitted to work for any government agency or civilian company that receives government contracts. They will not qualify for any benefit paid for by their fellow citizens via taxation except obvious situations such as utilizing public transportation for which they will pay anonymously like everyone else. In short, they will have committed their future existence to a kind of internal exile, cut off from the general benefits of the society they were unwilling to serve.

The second component: School vouchers

The second component of the 5th Pillar is a recommendation to establish a comprehensive national program of K-12 school vouchers, issued to the parent's of every child in America. These vouchers will be in the amount of $5,000 per student per year, and be comprised of a $3,000 grant from the federal budget, and a $2,000 grant from each parent's respective state budget. Parents will take these vouchers and use them to pay all or part of the educational expenses at the school of their choice.

A change in terminology

I recommend that the term "public" be changed to "government" when referring to schools run by the federal, state, or local governments. This is a nomenclature adjustment that clarifies the difference between government and privately run educational institutions.

Parents are the key

The key feature of this new national voucher program at the K-12 level, is that it both recognizes and returns primary responsibility for educating children to parents. This dynamic program accomplishes this dual goal by empowering parents with decision-making responsibilities, i.e. evaluating which school best meets the educational needs of their children, while at the same time providing parents with finances to pay for some or all of each of their children's education.

Financially it is practical, because $5,000 per student adds up to $100,000 per 20 students—the current classroom size desired by most teachers. Entrepreneurially-minded teachers could singly or jointly start a private school, and five teachers (plus the usual compliment of aids and parents who assist) could easily teach 100 students. The parent's $500,000 contribution would fully fund a quality education program.

If this voucher program becomes law, it will positively change our school system. Government schools will loose their nearmonopoly in determining what curriculum and activities students experience, because they will compete on a more equal footing with private schools and home schools.

After the new system is implemented, much of the funding for each school will come from parent's vouchers, so each school will have to be market oriented. Each school will be competing for the trust of each parent. Schools will have to prove to parent's satisfaction that they can provide the best educational opportunity for students.

The education market will function like all markets, and with time, some schools will gain better reputations than others and will be in demand, while others will fail and will close for lack of support. The value of the vouchers will grow with the cost of living, and the choices open to parents will be greater as the market responds to demand. Schools (whether government or private) will compete based on the excellence of their programs and personnel.

I further recommend that each government school have an active Junior ROTC program (at least at the high school level), and that each student be a part of the corps of cadets. This uniformity will impart a host of positive attributes to our young people, including a greater level of discipline and enhanced self-esteem, helping transform them into better citizens. Currently, about one thousand American high schools have high school ROTC programs so there is ample experience to draw upon during the coming transition.

Many parents are not satisfied with the current government school system, and will welcome these developments. However, if parents prefer a traditional civilian approach and atmosphere, they can choose a private school that offers whatever structure and curriculum they desire.

An additional recommendation for government schools regards the faculty: teachers will be given the option of "limited" military reserve or National Guard commissions or ranks, and will be paid according to their rank and time in service. Previous seniority will count and factored into assignments of rank and accompanying compensation packages. Veteran teachers will have the additional option of maintaining their current salary and benefits package. If these senior teachers are not retained in the district or state government school system, they will be given whatever retirement benefits they have accumulated at that time.

All teachers in government schools will have the option of maintaining or joining whatever unions currently exist, or of forming new unions, or of not being part of any union—their choice.

Every teacher's military responsibilities will be limited in that they will be commissioned in a special education category and will not be obligated for other military service, i.e. monthly or summer drills, or deployments. But any teachers who are qualified and desire to do so may opt for traditional reserve/guard commissions, and will be required to drill and serve as has been the case for decades. The advantage of this latter option will be additional service opportunities and additional pay and retirement benefits.

In most cases, this new system will give teachers a pay increase, and since military pay is uniform nation wide (adjusted for high cost of living areas as is normal for military personnel stationed in different areas now), all teachers will receive similar pay.

Government schoolteachers will also appreciate the fact that class size will be reasonable (generally around 20 students/classroom), and that they will be assisted by aids—many of which are MNS's serving their two years in the Department of Education.

In this quasi-military environment, students will be required to obey teachers and school rules, and most violence will be a thing of the past. Teaching excellence will be rewarded with recognition and promotion—as is the case in most military environments. All students will wear uniforms provided at government expense, and teachers will wear officer uniforms (at least once a week, depending on the policy of the school principal). Students not cooperating will be removed from the school and sent home to their parents who will have to shop for a different school. Parent options for incorrigible students may include government or private schools established with a "boot camp" format—especially geared to encourage an "attitude adjustment" for rebellious students.

Private schools will establish their own rules of conduct, but their teachers must be certified to the extent they are required to today, and students must perform at an objectively established standard in order for parents to receive the school vouchers the following year. The same standards will apply to those parents who home-school their children. Parents in this latter category will be granted significant latitude in justifying educational expenditures (i.e. field trips, school supplies, etc.) but their children must pass the same federal Department of Education tests to receive their vouches the next school year.

Importantly, there will be significant parental input to the national tests, including parent groups who elect to home school, and those who send their kids to private schools. Offensive questions with an anti-supernatural bias or anti-religious assumptions will be subject to review and probably removed from the tests. Test questions will focus on objective, quantitative data learned from a body of factual knowledge. Students will have memorized or learned to analyze facts during the previous term. Subjects emphasized will be math, history, English, and science. All students will be taught to read and write. All students will enjoy reasonably rigorous physical education including sports. Other subjects will be introduced or taught as time permits. Parents will be expected to seek out experiences for their kids in the arts and other "rounding out" endeavors as part of extra-curricular activities.

The voucher system may be adjusted for levels of student achievement (based on objective test scores) rather than simply being an "all or nothing" payment system. I am flexible in this recommendation and am open to innovative ideas that will help this new system flourish.

Some doubt that parents are up to the challenge

Some critics of home schooling challenge the capability and capacity of parents to educate their own children. First of all, it is the parent's responsibility to ensure that their children receive the best education possible (given individual time and budgetary constraints). Secondly, most parents care far more about their own children than do non-family members (professionally trained or not). Thirdly, proof of a student's achievement and a school's excellence will be scores on objective tests. If the home-schooled students don't measure up, their parents will not receive their vouchers for the next time period. The same standard will apply to private or government schools. But it is interesting to note that for the last several years, home-schooled students have won national spelling bees, scored high on SAT's, and been admitted to leading colleges and universities.

Preparation for National Service

The four years of high school should include mental, physical, and moral preparation for the upcoming term of required national service, and parents should insure that a combination of family, church, school and outside activities each contribute to developing a well-rounded young adult.

Within the academic portion, I recommend that a battery of tests be administered in high school to evaluate each student's suitability for various national service options. These tests should be part of an integrated system that encourages students to begin focusing on an area of government service appropriate for them when they graduate.

High school students should be given an opportunity to meet representatives from various government departments and agencies, and to view films, take field trips, etc., before their final national service assignment is made during their senior year. By then they will have a good idea of what options await, and they (and receiving government departments) can plan for their transition and training. Parents, teachers, and students will all have input in the final assignments, but ultimately, it is the individual recruit that will sign a contract with the government, and they will have to make the crucial decision of selecting from the list of options open to them at that time. I suggest that students be given their service choices by class rank—making the competition for choice more equitable, and adding a sense of urgency to academic excellence.

As is the case in military units today, I recommend that government schools include a chaplain on the faculty. This religious presence will have a positive effect on the school, and be a clear signal that God is once again respected by "the system". These clergy persons may be civilians from local congregations, or retired, former, or reserve military chaplains who have a great deal of experience in this rewarding calling and ministry.

Budget highlights of the MNS and voucher programs

- The number of students in each year group of the K-12 system is estimated at 4 million per year for a total of 52 million students. 95% of each graduation class is 3.8 million students. 5% is 200,000 students.
- Each parent will receive a $3,000 school voucher from the federal government for each of their K-12 students, and an additional $2,000 voucher from each state. Those parents living in states where the state government rejects this new program will not receive the federal portion. My prediction is that parents will vote for state leaders who support the new program.

- The initial (2005) federal portion of the voucher program budget will be $156 billion.
- The initial (2005) state's portion of the voucher program budget will be $104 billion.
- The annual budget for post-MNS education vouchers (for the veterans who complete their required two years of service) is $95 billion, plus normal inflation and cost of living increases.
- The budget for the 5% of students who qualify for, and elect to receive, the college ROTC scholarships (and who complete their four years of service) will begin at $4 billion annually, and then top out at $36 billion (2005 dollars), plus cost of living/inflation adjustments as necessary.
- Military Academy appointments will not count against the 5% totals, but annually, only about 3,000 freshmen enter the military academies. The budget for the academies is included in the base budget of the Department of Defense.
- College level schools will receive five years of special support from the federal government to compensate them for the loss of MNS personnel fulfilling their service requirements. The initial (2005) budget is $38 billion.

Summary

The magnitude of good that will result from universal mandatory national service and universal school vouchers is hard to calculate. Using the objective standard of a 40-hour workweek, MNS personnel will contribute **8 billion hours of service** the first year and **16 billion** thereafter! The amount of increased patriotism each person will experience as a result of their contributions is incalculable. Each citizen will really feel like they "own a piece of the rock!" School vouchers, in a tangible way, will return primary authority and responsibility to educate children to parents. Funding vouchers from combined federal and state budgets will reinforce our federalist system and strengthen the ties that bind our democracy together. MNS higher education vouchers will give a broader section of our citizenry a chance to attend college.

In the final analysis, everyone will benefit from these two programs. The only unknowns are the amounts of tangible and intangible or individual and collective benefits our society will receive from their service.

"I know that the Lord secures justice for the poor and upholds the cause of the needy."
Psalm 140:12

CHAPTER SIX

The 6th Pillar of Freedom: Health Care Reforms

Introduction

Though the American health care system provides the best technical medical care in the world today, it is also the most expensive, and its skyrocketing costs are threatening everyone. The 6th Pillar contains recommendations that will lower costs and bring currently uninsured citizens under an umbrella of basic protection.

Since malpractice litigation is one of the key factors negatively impacting our health care system, I recommend relieving doctors (and other health care professionals who currently buy malpractice insurance) from this burden. Health care costs are so high that, in the long run when you factor in Medicare costs that are specifically addressed in the 7th Pillar, they endanger our long-term solvency.

Reducing costs while increasing quality

Malpractice Insurance and Lawsuits

Currently, American physicians and other health care professionals are at risk from lawsuits every time they see a patient. This once most-trusted of all human relationships has been hurt by our increasingly litigious society, and the lure of large monetary awards for patients (and a few unscrupulous lawyers who exploit this broken system) has dramatically impacted costs. Costs are skyrocketing because all malpractice insurance premiums and jury awards are passed along to patients in the form of higher medical bills.

Some doctors spend more than $250,000 on annual malpractice insurance premiums, but tragically, even with these exorbitant premiums, many insurance companies are refusing to insure doctors because awards in malpractice cases are so high that insuring doctors is unprofitable. Because of this terrible situation, many doctors are leaving the profession or changing to other specialties.[1]

A solution that helps everyone

To solve this problem, I recommend that every medical professional that pays malpractice insurance be offered reserve military commissions in exchange for the federal government paying their malpractice premiums. This financial relief, combined with a change in how malpractice cases are handled and awards paid, will greatly lower the costs of American health care. Of perhaps greater importance, this new program will remove much of the adversarial relationship and lack of trust that has developed between our medical professionals who have devoted their lives to healing, and those of us in the general public who need their care.

Medical professionals choosing to take advantage of this offer will be required to make the same time commitment as other reservists: two days per month, and two weeks in the summer, plus national emergencies. But of great importance, they will usually be assigned (perhaps one half day per week) in their local community helping those without health insurance. This new system will provide a health care safety net and it will be funded by, and replace, the current Medicaid/SCHIP program, which I recommended for elimination in the 4th Pillar.

I call the new program USA Medical Care, and it is funded at the rate of $100 billion annually to start. I admit it is a socialistic program, but it follows with my philosophy of gradually phasing the larger socialistic programs out of our federal budget, without jerking the rug out from under the many that have become dependent on these services. I want this program to be viewed more as practical charity than a system seeking to forcibly redistribute wealth (my principle objection to overt socialism). In time, this new program may be phased-out or increased, as succeeding generations of citizens desire.

Those medical professionals electing to accept the government's offer may staff community health centers, which currently serve many (particularly poor or rural) patients. But this program is created not only to serve existing patients, but also that portion of our society that has no health insurance.

In return for their invaluable part-time military service, doctors and others in the program will be paid the same rate as all medical reservists (according to MOS, rank, etc.). This pay, when combined with the value of malpractice insurance premiums, will be very attractive to many. But more importantly to our greater society, many doctors will stay in professions and specialties they are increasingly vacating, and those in the general community who currently have no health insurance will be protected.

Practically, a small fee for service may be requested from each patient seeking treatment, but these fees will not be the principle source of program financing. Fees will be adjusted according to each person's ability to pay, and the extremely poor will pay nothing.

A safety net

During regular reserve military drills, medical professionals in the USA Medical Care program will be assigned duties by their chains of command, and many will serve in their own offices. This system will be a safety net for (currently) forty-five million Americans without health insurance, and it will work on a first come, first served basis. Throughout our history, many doctors have had charity clinics (sometimes weekly) where they treat the poor, so this system has honorable roots in our generous past.

This program is not intended to be comprehensive, socialized medicine, nor a single-payer system, nor a copy of any foreign system. It is just a practical program to provide health care for those in a temporary bind, or those immersed in long-term poverty that need help. Some people may elect to abandon their existing health care to try and save money by taking advantage of this system, but since its budget is limited, and typically will not be as thorough as paid health care, everyone will have to adjust accordingly. In the end, in America you get what you pay for, and that's the way it should always be in our society built on personal responsibility and liberty.

That said, I believe most Americans will not object to a small portion of the federal budget being expended to help fellow citizens and permanent residents (particularly children) who have no health care.

Reasonable efforts should be made to determine the identification of those requesting help, and if persons needing urgent care are determined to be in the country illegally, they should be mercifully treated, and then turned over to the proper authorities for deportation.

The necessity of starting a medical court system

The second component of this strategy to lower exorbitant health care costs requires changing our legal system. I support the popular idea that a special medical court system be developed to handle only medical cases. In these special medical courts, judges will be trained to work in conjunction with a panel of medical professionals— specialists who understand the intricacies of medical situations. Each judge and/or panel team will first be required to determine the relative merits of each malpractice case brought to the medical court, and either accept the case for trial, refer the case to the regular court system if appropriate, or dismiss the case for lack of merit.

In the course of the medical court's proceedings, if any medical professional is charged with a capital crime such as murder, they will be remanded to the criminal court system for trial, sentencing, and punishment. But those proved to have made accidental medical errors, or judged to be incompetent, or to be guilty of a medical ethics violation, will remain in the medical court system to either be de-licensed until they receive retraining, or permanently removed from the profession. Victims will be compensated fairly, according to new objective guidelines applying to each type of case.

Limiting compensation

Medical court judges will direct insurance companies to pay restitution to victims according to the relevant applicable policies, but the amounts of the awards will be limited and paid according to new exacting formulas. All awards will be paid promptly, and a special panel of experts will establish fair insurance premiums for the government to pay on behalf of medical professionals in the USA Medical Care program (as well as medical professionals who practice independently or are in other systems such as health maintenance organizations—HMO's). This panel of experts will factor in victim's needs, insurance company costs and reasonable profits, actuarial tables, and reasonable legal fees.

Capping Awards and Legal Fees

I recommend placing a cap or ceiling on monetary awards to victims. A panel of medical experts, legal professionals from the new medical court system, victim's rights organizations, and other relevant parties will develop the objective criteria for these caps. These criteria will guide the judge as he or she determines the proper award for each case, and factor in many variables including severity of injuries, how many productive years the victim has remaining, and other relevant considerations. Other costs may be added to economic damages, including special equipment needs, nursing or home care requirements, and so forth. Juries will not be part of the medical court system.

I recommend that economic damages not exceed one thousand five hundred dollars per week (plus inflation) for the remaining life of the victim, plus the special needs requirements mentioned above. These weekly payments will come from the insurance company, but may be creatively financed from the purchase of government bonds or other innovative ideas developed in the future.[2]

I also recommend limiting legal fees to not more than one thousand dollars per day (including class action cases), per lawyer, per case. This breaks down to $125 per hour, per eight-hour day, per legal professional—a generous wage by most American's standards. Legal fees will only be paid for actual case preparation and trial time. Full payment of legal fees will be made from the insurance award at the time of the initial insurance payment.

Judges will assign public defenders to victims unable to afford a privately funded lawyer, and these lawyers should remain with their client after the medical court's initial screening determines that the case has enough merit to be worthy of moving forward for trial.

Anyone making a false accusation against a medical professional will be remanded to the criminal court system for trial and punishment. But all persons who honestly believe they have been wronged will be encouraged to lodge a complaint with the medical court. Every medical facility will be required to advise patients of their rights to complain to the medical court system (perhaps when signing in for examinations or treatment).

Medical licenses

Initial licensing would continue as is the practice today, but professional panels would screen medical professionals every four or five years thereafter when they come up for licensing review. These panels would evaluate the proficiency of every professional against objective standards established for each specialty or medical profession. They would then have the option of either granting the individual another license (perhaps for a longer term), or they could assign retraining, or even refuse to grant another license—as appropriate. Standards would be objective, but judgments would be subject to appeal to an appellate medical court—with rules consistent throughout the United States.

Employer provided health benefits

In an effort to help the health care industry be more marketoriented, employers should be forbidden from forcing employees to use a certain health care provider. Employers should be required to compensate employees with cash payments for their health care insurance as part of offered compensation packages (to the extent health care benefits are part of offered compensation).

Employees will then take their cash to the health care insurance marketplace, and purchase whatever policy they desire (given individual budget constraints). They may elect "fee-for-service" medical care and have full freedom to do so. The market will adjust to this new competitive environment, and health care costs will drop accordingly.

A better system

Other than the changes recommended above, the best of our current system should remain as it is. Members of the medical community may hang out their own shingle or work for HMO's or hospitals or wherever they choose or can get hired. The only differences will be that health care costs will be significantly reduced, and the attractiveness of the medical profession will be significantly enhanced. Practically, no one will be without basic health care, and the government will have an increased pool of doctors to help in national emergencies.

Medical professionals will have the option of being relieved of the burden of malpractice insurance, and all medically related lawsuits will be screened for merit. All citizens/permanent residents will have basic medical care available, and an energized medical profession to help them.

Patients will additionally benefit because unnecessary procedures and tests will no longer be ordered just so doctors can protect themselves from possible lawsuits. In other words, medical professionals will no longer have to practice medicine while looking over their shoulder. The annual savings from eliminating unnecessary tests is estimated at more than $100 billion—an amount that will meet most of the costs necessary to pay for the new USA Medical Care program. These savings will also contribute to establishing and maintaining the new medical court system described above.[3]

Monthly discussion panels organized by the medical court in each geographical area will provide opportunities for every medical professional to learn about problems that are reaching 'their' court system, and enjoy discussions with their colleagues to improve medical skills in a non-threatening environment. Doctors and others will be able to discuss mistakes and to learn from them—vital to great patient care.

Prescription drug policy

Before leaving the health care sector, I want to address the issue of prescription drugs, another vital and hot button issue today. Medicine is expensive and getting more so, and seniors, more than most, are seemingly caught in the middle. That is part of the reason I recommend granting $12,000 (cash—tax-free) in annual Medicare benefits to current and soon to be retiring seniors. However, certain critics of the American system advocate buying drugs from Canada or elsewhere in an attempt to get the same drugs at lower costs. But there are dangers to this strategy—as the following points make clear.

Drugs obtained from Canada do not have the backing of the Canadian government. These drugs may be "expired...appear to be counterfeit, and are less than the prescribed dosage".[4]

Also, when the government interferes in the prescription drug market via price controls, it could hurt drug quality by undermining American drug companies' research and development budgets. Additionally, intellectual property rights could be seriously infringed, further impacting the quality of our own drugs and the companies who produce them.[5]

The United States has the best prescription drugs on the planet, and "the U.S. accounts for 53 percent of the R&D in the world".[6] Let's be very careful to look at the big picture and nurture this vital domestic industry for our mutual good. As soon as the recommendations included in the 4th and 6th Pillars are implemented, prices for all health care related products and services will go down, and seniors will have significant tax-free incomes to spend as they choose on health care.

Summary

In summary, the reforms recommended in the 6th Pillar of Freedom will reduce the overall costs of health care in America, increase the accountability and standards of all health care professionals, and provide health care coverage for every citizen and permanent legal resident. Medicine will be free of the dark cloud currently casting a shadow over this great profession — a time-honored profession that benefits everyone in our society.

Additionally, those medical professionals electing to participate in the USA Medical Care program will be available to help our national defense and emergency response organizations, and will be relieved of terrible economic and professional burdens. These improvements will ensure that the American health care system continues to improve and evolve in a positive atmosphere of mutual trust and respect.

Notes

(1) *Time magazine*, June 9, 2003. The article is entitled "The Doctor Won't See You Now: The Soaring Cost of Malpractice." Please refer to related articles in the same issue, especially the table at the bottom of page 55.

(2) Ibid. The article suggests that the doctor's insurance company pay for the purchase price of the bonds. When the person dies, the bonds will go into the deceased person's estate. If the person survives until the bonds mature, the final yield may be reinvested or the lump sum may go directly to the beneficiary. Damages for non-economic injuries, usually called pain and suffering awards, will be capped at $250,000.

(3) Ibid.

(4) *President's Message: Newsletter of the Pacific Research Institute*, Summer 2004, article by PRI president and CEO Sally C. Pipes, "Play it safe with healthcare", pages 1-2. Ms.

Pipes is discussing research done by Rudolph Giuliani, former mayor of New York City. I recommend that everyone interested in public policy, whether in education, healthcare, or free markets, visit the PRI website at www.pacificresearch.org, and support their good work as best you can.

(5) Ibid. (6) Ibid.

"Lord, you have assigned me my portion and my cup; you have made my lot secure. The boundary lines have fallen for me in pleasant places; surely I have a delightful inheritance."
Psalm 16:5-6

CHAPTER SEVEN

The 7th Pillar of Freedom: Social Security and Medicare Reforms

Introduction

I f Social Security and Medicare are truly the "third rails" of American public policy, then our country is headed for bankruptcy.[1] Social Security and Medicare are the largest combined component of our federal budget, and they will be the largest drag on our economy during the next seventy-five years. The long-term budget projections in the 4th Pillar indicate that without the changes recommended in this chapter (or similar changes such as those recommend by Professor Laurence Kotlikoff in *Generational Storm*) the country will experience tens of trillions in budgetary shortfall, and eventual financial collapse.

These programs have grown into massive socialistic entitlements, but in good faith, despite my long-term desire to eliminate socialistic elements from our society and federal budget, we should maintain our obligation to meet our promises to current and soonto-be retirees. These seniors are counting on payments from the Social Security and Medicare systems to help them live out their days in independence and good health.

In the 7th Pillar I present fair and balanced solutions that will help us avoid long-term financial disaster, while at the same time, generously funding the needs of current and "Baby Boom" generation retirees. Both entitlement programs will be funded for everyone up to and including those who turn 65 in 2020. But everyone turning 65 in year-groups 2021 through 2052 will experience gradual reduction in program benefits.

And finally, those who turn 65 in year 2053 and following, are on notice now that they have their entire adult working lives to prepare for their retirements, and if they arrive at age 65 destitute, they will have to rely on family, friends, or charity to survive. Good stewardship dictates that they save wisely for the future.

Please refer to the seventy-five year budget projection at the end of chapter four to see the positive long-term economic benefits of phasing out these programs. However, please note that every qualifying beneficiary will be paid as long as they live, and it is possible that some retirees will still be alive and receiving benefits until sometime early in the 22nd Century.

A gradual phase out

In 2021 (the first year that 65-year-old retirees will be impacted by the 3% per year phase out) retiree's will receive 97% of the Social Security and Medicare benefits they would have received otherwise. Payments (adjusted for inflation) will then steadily decrease at a continual rate of 3% for each subsequent year-group turning 65, until benefits are completely eliminated for people turning 65 in 2053 (kids who are 16 today).

When the last of the long line of beneficiaries dies about one hundred years from now, both programs will finally end. However the positive impact of the phase out will be seen in our federal budget from 2021 onwards—just 16 years from now.

Background

How did America get to the point where we have massive socialistic entitlement programs that absorb 50% of our federal budget, programs now forcing us to face a long-term $51 trillion revenue shortfall? This situation began in the darkest days of the Great Depression in the 1930's when many seniors faced destitution. President Franklin Roosevelt proposed, and congress enacted, legislation that founded the Social Security system. This generosity was never intended to be the massive federal entitlement program we have today, but rather was envisioned as a safety net to be placed under seniors to help their few last days be manageable and dignified. (Medicare was enacted later but exerts the greatest pressure on our long-term economic health).

However, enacting entitlement legislation was far easier than funding it. As the years went by and demographics dramatically changed, these new programs began exerting inordinate financial pressures on our economy and budget. They will continue to accelerate, and will eventually swamp our ship of state in a sea of red ink.

Unexpected demographic changes

The leaders who founded these programs didn't place strict constraints on expansion, nor did they envision the dramatic changes in our demographics that occurred after World War II.

When Social Security was instituted in the mid-1930s, the ratio of working people to retirees was about 16 to 1. The system was structured so that current workers paid a portion of their wages into a trust fund, creating an accumulating "pool" of funds to pay benefits to workers when they retired. A multi-generational deal was struck, whereby each working generation contributed to the retired generation ahead of it, with the expectation that each following generation would also provide the same courtesy.

Unfortunately, several problems occurred during the intervening years that placed this structure in jeopardy. First, Congress didn't let the funds accumulate. Over the years, our lawmakers decided to utilize them for other purposes (in addition to paying retiree's), and they dipped into these payroll funds and spent the money for other purposes. In the place of the "borrowed" payroll funds, congress left behind bonds—IOU's that must be funded from general tax revenues in future federal budgets.

Additionally, Social Security's founder's utilized demographic projections that assumed the same high worker to retiree ratio mentioned above. They did not foresee that the 16 to 1 ratio would evaporate as dramatically as it has. The ratio has now dropped to about 3 to 1, and within a few years it will drop to 2 to 1. And when the current growth projections in entitlement benefits (especially health care), are compared to the flatter growth projections in federal revenue, the system is in serious trouble because the revenue gap widens dramatically—and soon. Social Security and Medicare are unsustainable at current rates if two workers are expected to support each retiree.

Besides the miscalculations regarding the worker to retiree ratio, initial planners didn't (and couldn't) foresee the incredible growth in our population during the baby boom generation, followed by an equally dramatic drop during the "baby bust" generation. The latter's trend has been accelerated by the massive number of abortions.

Also unforeseen by the founders was the incredible lengthening of adult life span. Today, the **average** person living to age 65 is projected to live to age 90! This means that instead of caring for a retiree for 5 years, the two entitlement programs must care for them for 25 years. This is wonderful in one sense, and a financial disaster in another!

Non-solutions

1. Massive tax hikes

Budget wise, if we maintain the same income tax and payroll tax systems that we have today, the only way current and future retirees can be provided with promised benefits is to institute immediate and massive raises in all tax rates. These massive rate hikes will include individual and corporate income taxes, the various payroll taxes, and every other type of tax creative politicians can think up.

However, this "solution" presents an additional problem: if these tax hikes are enacted, they will be so large that they will overwhelm productivity. Workers are hard-pressed now. Is it reasonable to believe that everyone will be able to handle across-the-board tax hikes that require everyone to pay more to the government than we take home? There won't be enough money left in worker's paychecks to sustain their families.

2. Printing more money

To avoid these massive tax hikes, another proposed "solution" is for the federal government to print massive waves of new currency. But $51 trillion dollars in cheap currency will collapse the dollar's value, rendering it worthless. We only have to turn to Germany following World War I to witness a classic example of worthless currency created by the "printing press" approach. During that monetary crisis it took a wheelbarrow load of nearly worthless cash to buy a loaf of bread. There are other international examples of hyperinflation, including recent economic crises in Brazil and Argentina where this approach also failed.

No, flooding the economy with worthless dollars will only hasten our economic demise. This solution is just as bad as taxing the living daylights out of current and succeeding generations of workers. So, if we can't tax our way out of the impending crises, nor print our way out, the only logical solution is to reduce our debts and obligations and/or increase our revenue.

Healthy solutions

I propose we do both — solutions that are practical and "doable" and have two components. The first was presented in the 4th Pillar — replacing the current income tax system with a national retail sales tax system, with an initial tax rate sufficient to bring in enough revenue to pay our bills and pay off our debts.

The second solution is considered here. We must reform our Social Security and Medicare entitlement programs — utilizing the multi-generational exit strategy mentioned above.

My basic philosophical tenant is to treat each retiree as an individual, but retirees who share income will be required to claim their portion (for married couples this usually means an equal share) when requesting retirement benefits. Obviously, qualifying married couples who are both retired will receive two sets of paychecks and there is no built-in marriage penalty.

Next I recommend that, starting immediately, all retiree's receive their benefits at age 65. Gone will be the options of receiving reduced benefits starting at age 62, or receiving increased benefits by waiting longer. This change will impact folks in various ways: some retiree's will get more benefits but will have to wait longer, while others will receive less benefits but will get them sooner. But under the new system, everyone will receive the same flat rate — subject to a sliding scale based on individual income (sometimes refered to as means-testing).

Benefits

The recommended rates are as follows: Social Security will pay a maximum of $1,500 per month to all individual retirees who make less than $50,000 per year (currently, 75% of Americans receive incomes of less than $50,000 annually). Importantly, this provision applies only to "take-home" income under the new Dynamic Tax system, and has nothing to do with a person's assets. You may arrive at age 65 as a millionaire or destitute, but it is your income that will be applied to the "means-testing" mechanism used to calculate your Social Security and Medicare checks.

Those individual retirees (and others currently covered by the Old Age, Survivors, and Disability Insurance program) who take home between $50,000 and $99,000 annually, will receive 2% less for each $1,000 of annual income. Individual retiree's whose annual income is $100,000 or more will receive no benefits that year.

Medicare benefits will be $1,000 per month per retiree. The same age and income requirements will apply as with Social Security. Please note: though in the budget calculations I have kept these programs separate, it does make sense to combine them and issue eligible retirees one check monthly. An added benefit in combining the two programs will be administrative cost savings which leads to lower taxes.

The maximum combined individual retirement check will be $2,500 per month per individual. This equals $30,000 per retiree per year or $60,000 per couple per year. All things considered, this is a pretty generous retirement package for a couple that may arrive at age 65 with nothing. It is a generous provision from a generous society. Importantly, Social Security and Medicare benefits will not be considered in the income calculation—only non-benefit income will determine program paychecks.

Administration

As retirees approach their individual 65th birthday and have calculated that their projected individual net income is less than $100,000, they may contact their Social Security/Medicare office and submit their application for benefits. Each applicant will be asked to present their income documents, proof of age and identity, etc. Others qualifying for benefits (as is the case under the current program) may contact their Social Security office at any time as they become eligible.

Following initial induction into the retirement system, each retiree must submit an annual estimated income form and other documents as required. Even if they did not qualify for benefits when they turned 65 (due to incomes above the allowable annual level), if a retiree's financial situation deteriorates for any reason in subsequent years, they may apply for benefits at that time. When their estimated (and verified) income drops below the maximum threshold, they will be entitled to appropriate benefits.

It is important to note that both Social Security and Medicare payments will be based on the income estimates made by retiree's at the beginning of each retirement year. The income declaration must be signed by both the retiree and a CPA level accountant, and then subsequently verified to the reasonable extent possible by their case officer. Lying on these government forms will be a federal offence, and will be penalized by (at least) loss of benefits.

Summary

Before Social Security and Medicare programs stop accepting new retirees in 2053, all persons who retire will be amply and fairly provided for out of the federal treasury for the rest of their lives. Many retirees' will receive higher levels of benefits than they might have received under the current system, and some will receive less (wealthy persons individually making $100,000 or more will receive no benefits) but it is a fair system that phases out over nearly one hundred years.

Any loss of benefits must be balanced with the comprehensive financial gains made possible under the new Dynamic Tax system, where all income taxes, estate taxes, capital gains taxes, and other current taxes have been eliminated. All well-to-do retiree's will only pay normal sales taxes like everyone else—and even these rates will gradually diminish over time.

This balanced system is as reasonable as I can make it, and accomplishes the dual purposes of providing amply for current and soon-to-be retirees, while at the same time gradually eliminating these massive socialistic entitlement programs from our federal budget. I sincerely hope that most seniors consider this a fair deal and a fair trade—both for themselves and the country they have faithfully served.

Notes

1. Please read *The Coming Generational Storm*, cited earlier. Professor Kotlikoff warns that in the long run, without significant changes, America is heading for a $51 trillion dollar revenue shortfall—which is obvious bankruptcy.

CHAPTER EIGHT

Additional Issues

Introduction

A merica is a complex society facing many important and controversial issues. Before closing I wanted to address some of these issues, going on the record out of respect for their relative importance.

As with the 7 Pillars, each issue reflects only my opinion rather than certain objective truth. My choices are as follows:

Racism. Though clearly sinful, human beings have looked down on one other for different reasons since the Fall. But since race is such an integral and visible part of each person's being, racial prejudices are more easily acquired, dividing us along racial lines. The Bible teaches that God in his wisdom and love assigned race or ethnicity to each person he created. To Him, each of us has unique value, and each of us can please Him equally if we do so on the basis of His revealed objective truth in the scriptures.

All of us are born into varying circumstances, but none of us are without responsibility to make the most of who we are and what gifts we have been given. As a result of this philosophy, I support laws that facilitate individual liberty and responsibility, laws that support initiative and excellence—a naturally level playing field, not an artificial one.

Whether this philosophy of individual responsibility is applied to racial or ethnic considerations in academia, the military, business, the arts, or whatever component of society we strive in, I want true freedom to rule within the constraints of the open market of competition and ideas.

Two concrete examples where race and ethnicity have factored into government criterion include university acceptance and business contracts. I advocate changing our system so that objective criteria form the basis of the selection procedures for both sectors.

Anyone who is intelligent and works hard and earns the right to be in the top five percent of all applicants will be given potential access to our top universities via the ROTC scholarships. Each applicant should be accepted or rejected based objective performance standards, regardless of race or ethnicity. I am against granting less qualified students access to limited university slots because of racial quotas. Obviously possessing unusual talents should be part of the objective consideration criterion, so that athletes with 3.5 GPA's may be granted slots instead of one-dimensional academic types with sterling GPA's.

These standards should especially apply to sectors funded by the people's tax dollars. However, if a private college is funded without tax dollars, they should have every right to admit students on whatever basis they choose (once they complete their MNS requirements).

Similarly, I am against racial or ethnic based set-asides and quotas for businesses competing for government contracts. Objective standards such as proven excellence and bid quotes should be the determining factors in awarding contracts.

If private individuals or entities decide to fund scholarships or hire certain individuals or companies because of a personal desire to compensate for the past sins of our nation (particularly slavery), then they should have freedom to do so. But the practice of penalizing the current generation of innocent citizens for the sins of the past is contrary to the American ideal of fairness. We will inherit the lingering consequences of past sins, but we should not inherit the penalties.

This balanced approach will send a clear message to everyone in our society that we must all must compete based on objective standards and production rather than quotas.

It is true that, to some extent, we reap what we sow, and Americans will have to bear the burden of racial tension for a few more generations. But that said, the best long-term solution to racism is to allow everyone to compete in the market place of excellence. In the long run, drive, initiative, and productivity carry the day.

The Federal Marriage Amendment (FMA). Currently, codifying the sanctity of marriage is one of the hottest societal issues facing America, an issue that addresses the very nature of the family, and its future in America. The FMA is an issue because elements within our society support homosexuality, and are forcing us to consider their demands that behavior and relationships forbidden in the Bible be legalized and given the same status as heterosexual marriage and family.

It is important to stress that every sin can be forgiven, and if you are uncertain about biblical teaching regarding the sinfulness of homosexuality, please read Leviticus 18:22 and 20:13 in the Old Testament, and Romans 1:26-27 in the New Testament. That said, whoever repents is forgiven according to God's promise in 1 John 1:9.

Since privacy is also a legitimate issue in our constitution and society, I am not advocating that sexual acts between consenting adults in the privacy of their own homes or places of lodging be subject to intrusive laws. There are privacy implications here that cover both the righteous and the sinful. But certainly American society, based as it is on our biblical, Judeo-Christian heritage, can address this and any moral issue.

I am especially concerned that we protect vulnerable minors from any form of homosexual exploitation by predatory adults. Exploitation or rape should be punished equally harshly, whether the crimes involve hetero or homosexual criminals.

With this philosophical discussion as my preamble, I want to express full support for the Federal Marriage Amendment. In essence, it states that marriage in America will only be recognized if it is between one man and one woman at one time. This precludes the legality both homosexual and polygamous unions.

Immigration. There are two issues here: securing our borders, and establishing and enforcing clear laws to determine who can live here and under what circumstances. We must stop both illegal immigration and border penetration, and reform our legal immigration criteria.

Surely it is beyond controversy in the post 9/11 era that we must secure our borders. There is much history and many excuses why our borders are so porous now, but no excuse is acceptable, and no situation is unsolvable.

If lack of personnel is the main issue, then the new MNS laws presented in the 5th Pillar will help solve that dilemma. If budget is the problem, then the increased revenue and adjusted budgeting priorities presented in the 4th Pillar provide that solution. Let us quickly and efficiently figure out what needs to be done and do it! A few suggestions:

The first step in securing our borders is to mobilize enough homeland security and/or military troops, and move them into strategic positions to seal every illegal crossing area. Next, government and/or civilian engineers must design a continuous physical barrier, complete with adequate fencing, open areas, and guard towers to keep all unwanted intruders at bay. This is not rocket science—it just takes personnel, engineering, financing and a comprehensive construction plan to complete the job. Coast Guard and Navy assets must be similarly mobilized to guarantee protection of our coastal areas, inland waterways, and adjacent sea-lanes and airspace.

The second issue is legal immigration. We are a nation of immigrants so we have every reason to be philosophically open to lawabiding international citizens who want to come here and throw in their lot with us. But that said, we are obligated to determine who we want to come here, and on what basis they will be admitted. We must objectively determine which foreigners (and how many) will make the best contributions to our ever-progressing history.

Regarding numbers: America has an established history, general culture, language, and worldview, and a panel of experts on cultural absorption should be formed to help the immigration authorities determine the optimum number of immigrants we can absorb and acculturate. We want people to come here to join us, not turn us into a different country.

We should have a clear set of priorities of whom we would like to admit. Highly educated people with desirable skills, or successful entrepreneurs who will invest here and create new wealth for existing citizens, are examples of desirable immigrants. Spouses of American citizens should always be given special priority— admitted after the normal security checks. (My wife came here as a married immigrant, and it was truly ridiculous how protracted the immigration procedures were. She had to wait six months after our application was completed just to be granted an interview. This is not the way to engender good feelings between citizens and their government).

Additionally, we should always be open to exceptions to our quota policy. Foreigners, who are in grave personal danger due to undeserved religious or political persecution, should be admitted if they pose no threat. Waves of economic refugees must be kept at bay.

Lastly, we should establish clear guidelines and procedures for accepting short-term workers such as seasonal agricultural workers from Latin America, or engineers from India and elsewhere—both categories of which are so prevalent here in California (and generally good for our state and nation). We need foreign workers to do every job that we can't do ourselves—but we must establish clear protocols that admit and return workers in an organized, efficient, polite, and respectful manner. Obviously having secure borders will solve much of the "undocumented alien" problems, and eliminate our periodic amnesty contortions.

These simple changes will solve our current immigration crises and end status confusion for U.S. citizens and foreigners alike.

Unions and Management. I love working Americans and it is a constant source of frustration to me that workers and management live in seemingly endless tension. Maybe this is just the nature of the business world, but it seems to me that we could develop objective and transparent compensation and benefits formulas that would be acceptable to everyone.

Regarding unions, their leadership must be good stewards of worker's dues and contributions. We all know that, in the past, there have been some corrupt officials who have misused union funds. Also, union funds have been spent on political advertising that is contrary to the wishes of the rank and file.

Union officials must be transparently accountable for their management practices, and I support setting aside a portion of each member's contribution to be earmarked for public advocacy — but only if a mechanism is developed whereby each member can determine how his or her individual portion is spent.

Regarding management, these skilled leaders should get full marks for the burdens they bear on behalf of workers and owners (stockholders), and the accountability they have to the government. But the latest CEO to worker pay ratio has just been released (for fall, 2004) and company leaders of firms that employ greater than 500 workers now make more than 300 times the wages paid to their lowest paid (American) employees. That is out of proportion and should be brought within reason. I have no problem with company leadership making an inordinate return on personally invested capital, but I do have a problem with skewed salaries that give a rank and file worker $40,000 per year, and the company CEO $12 million per year.

Even more aggravating is when senior management decides to lay off workers to lower costs, but do so without taking significant pay cuts themselves (the essence of sacrificial leadership by example).

Pornography. This is another significant problem in America. Any form of sexually explicit material developed for lascivious or exploitative purposes should be illegal, but material utilizing the human body or form that is created for truly artistic or medical purposes should remain legal.

The Environment. God created the earth and everything in it. Therefore it makes good sense (and is commanded stewardship) to take good care of our planet. We have come a long way in the last forty years, steadily cleaning up our air and water—and that is great news (for a look at encouraging results after a generation of improvements, please see the annual *Index of Environmental Indicators,* written by Steven Hayward PhD., and published by Pacific Research Institute—website cited earlier).

Our air, water, and lands are much cleaner than they have been since the worst effects of the industrial revolution impacted the environment more than one hundred years ago. But those successes notwithstanding, much remains to be done. I encourage every individual, community, and nation to commit or recommit themselves to good environmental stewardship.

Sports. I wanted to end this section on a lighter note, and sports are definitely fun. But at the same time, sports are important in our culture and in most cultures around the world. Specifically, I have a couple of recommendations that I believe will help the "big four" American sports leagues (NFL, MLB, NHL, and NBA).

First, within each of the four leagues, the owners should pool their combined revenues from all sources. This change would make winning championships more a matter of player/coaching skill, than owner generosity. Any profits could also be split evenly. In other words, I advocate transforming sport franchises from primarily market-oriented competitive enterprises, to community cultures passed from one privileged steward to another.

Secondly, I recommend that all players be paid according to objective standards. Compensation would come from two sources: first, a pay chart must be devised that compensates depending on seniority. Quarterbacks and linemen would receive the same seniority pay. Perhaps players could be given $100,000 as rookies, followed by raises in $200,000 increments until players reached the apex of their careers. After that, they would receive equal decreases until they reached a veteran minimum at some future point when their level of play had diminished—but they were still making a contribution on the field and bringing delight to the fans.

The second objective source of player compensation would come from personal achievement—statistical productivity at their assigned position. Each player position would have points assigned that would fairly compare with other positions within that sport, and each player would be paid so much a point. For example, each homerun in baseball would be worth $100,000, each single worth $25,000, each goal or touchdown or triple-double, block that led to a touchdown, etc., be worth a certain monetary amount per point.

This dual compensation track would eliminate most controversy, holdouts, confusion, or legal wrangling. All would be paid according to the pay chart and production levels. These rules would not apply to individual sports like golf, nor to the amount of off-the-field compensation a player could receive from endorsements, etc.

To really stick my neck out, I would like to recommend two specific rule changes in baseball (our American pastime), both effecting umpires. First, the intentional walk rule should be changed to require the batter to be awarded second base instead of first. To enforce this rule, umpires would be given the responsibility of determining if a pitcher was trying to disguise an intentional walk with bad pitches. Situations would no doubt figure in umpire's decisions. Call this the "Barry Bonds" rule or whatever you like, it would dramatically improve the excitement of the game.

The second recommendation regards calling balls and strikes. This should be determined electronically, a technical innovation that would transform the incredibly subjective strike zone into an objective one. It is technically possible to implant a transmitter inside a baseball which can be detected by sensors placed in home plate and sewn into player's uniforms. These sensors would then create the true three-dimensional strike zone every player and fan has wanted for more than a hundred years. Umpires would call the game based on a handheld device indicating pitch location, and they would still decide other subjective aspects of the game such as beating out ground balls, etc.

The end result of these two changes would be a more definitive game. Umpires would gain some responsibility and loose some, but players and the fans would be happier.

Thus ends my foray into the world of sports administration.

Conclusion

The 7 Pillars of freedom will indeed positively impact America and the world. All that lies between our current situation and these policies being adopted into US law is for committed citizens to champion them and spread the word. We need determined people to step up and let our representatives at all levels of government know what changes we want. And if they don't share our vision, we need a new generation of Americans to be willing to run for office themselves and bring the 7 Pillars into law.

Our determination and excitement will grow as we envision what life will be like here and around the world once the pillars are established: Children will be safe from implantation through birth; Crime will largely be a phenomenon of the past; We will be able to travel most anywhere on the planet without fear, and ordinary citizens living in formally oppressive regimes will be consolidating their new freedoms with peace and joy; New tax laws will have brought improved prosperity for all Americans, and everyone will have greater responsibility for self-governance, and personal independence in financial matters and in day-to-day living; Doctors and patients will have renewed relationships based on mutual trust and professionalism, health care costs will have dropped, and all people will have basic medical coverage; And finally, seniors will have greater financial security, and greater assurance that their futures will be preserved and protected for the rest of their lives, and young people will have their entire working lives to prepare an excellent retirement.

These are bright hopes offered by the 7 Pillars of Freedom, and if we join together with common vision and persistence, we who support these policies will see better days ahead in the greatest country on earth.

About the Author

I hail from the Monterey Peninsula, in California, references to which are imbedded throughout my writings. I was born in Carmel, but lived the first few years of my life in an unincorporated area of nearby Seaside until my father and a few other local businessmen formed the new hamlet of Sand City. In 1962, when I was ten, my parents built a house in the pine forest in the hills between Carmel and Monterey, and I was privileged to live there until departing for my third year of college in 1972.

I was educated in public schools until my first graduate program, and eventually received graduate degrees from Canadian Theological Seminary (in Regina, Saskatchewan), the Graduate Theological Union (in Berkeley, California), and San Jose State University, and did doctoral work in history at the Vietnam Center at Texas Tech University. At Tech I was very fortunate to study with Professors Douglas Pike and James Reckner, both famous scholars specializing in US/Vietnam history—my academic field.

I served as a U.S. Army chaplain for fourteen years—six on active duty and eight in the Reserves and California National Guard. My highest rank was major, and my highest decoration was the Meritorious Service Medal.

I have two grown sons (who have wonderful wives and two children each) and my wife Becky and I have two young sons. We live in California.

Thank you for reading my book, and please join me in remembering that God **is** blessing America!

CPSIA information can be obtained
at www.ICGtesting.com
Printed in the USA
LVOW11s0637060717

540419LV00002B/294/P